By Christopher Dow

Fiction

Effigy
    Book I: Stroud
    Book II: Oakdale
The Books of Bob
    Devil of a Time
    Jumping Jehovah
The Clay Guthrie Mysteries
    The Dead Detective
    Landscape with Beast
    The Texas Troll Unlimited
    Darkness Insatiable
Roadkill
The Werewolf and Tide, and Other Compulsions

Nonfiction

Lord of the Loincloth (nonfiction novel)
Book of Curiosities: Adventures in the Paranormal
Occasional Pilgrimage: Essays on Film, Literature, and Other Matters
Living the Story: The Meandering, True, and Sometimes Strange
      Adventures of an Unknown Writer, Vols. I & II

Poetry

City of Dreams
The Trip Out
Texas White Line Fever
Networks
A Dilapidation of Machinery
Puzzle Pieces: Selected Poems

Art

Harboring with Arabesques: The Art of Christopher Dow

Martial Arts

The Wellspring: An Inquiry into the Nature of Chi
Circling the Square: Observations on the Dynamics of Tai Chi Chuan
Elements of Power: Essays on the Art and Practice of Tai Chi Chuan
Alchemy of Breath: An Introduction to Chi Kung
Leaves on the Wind: A Survey of Martial Arts Literature, Vols. I–VI

Editor

Drifts: Texas Writers: Interviews and Profiles
The Abby Stone: The Poetry of Bartholo Dias
The Best of Phosphene
The Best of Dialog

The Best of
PHOSPHENE

The Best of
PHOSPHENE

Compiled and Edited by
Christopher Dow

Phosphene Publishing Company
Temple, Texas

The Best of Phosphene
© 2026
ISBN: 979-8-9914875-3-5

"Foreword"
© 2026 by Christopher Dow

The individual poems, works of fiction, and essays
contained in this collection
© 2026 by their authors.

Phosphene was published in 1978 and 1979 by
Phosphene Publishing Company, Houston, Texas.

Published by
Phosphene Publishing Company
Temple, Texas
www.phosphenpress.com

Cover: Reproduced from the cover of the original
publication of *Phosphene* #1, by Randy Hajovsky

1.1 (1/2/26)

Contents

Fiction

Essays

The Best of
PHOSPHENE

Foreword

IF I KNEW THEN WHAT I know now. . . .

Can any statement be more fraught with ambiguity? Most commonly, people use it to express regret at a past course of action, such as, "If I knew that *Phosphene* would be so short-lived and cost me so much effort and money, I might never have published it."

The flip side is more complex, and maybe that's why people usually don't mean the statement in a positive way. But ultimately, *Phosphene* was one of the best things I ever did.

Phosphene was Houston's first independent literary and arts magazine, by which I mean it wasn't connected to a local university or writers' group. The first seeds of its creation were sowed, though I didn't realize it at the time, in about 1972. At the time, I was college junior, sitting in the back of a pickup truck in the parking lot of a laundromat in the Montrose Area, waiting for my clothes to finish drying and enjoying the balmy afternoon. I was writing in my notebook and trying to figure out what I was going to do with my life. I was fast approaching the end of a tentative and problematic undergraduate career at the University of Houston, where I was an English major with aspirations to be a professional writer.

Even that early, I had become aware of just how difficult being a professional writer could be—enough rejection slips to fill a shoebox had clearly and bluntly made the point—and I knew I had to find an appropriate avenue of approach on a very limited map. One way to support myself as a writer might have been to remain in school and become a university professor, but I had absolutely no desire to teach. Unfortunately, my refusal to go the teaching route seemed to remove about half the opportunities available, and the other half—becoming a reporter, advertising copy writer, or technical writer—seemed even worse. I never wanted to be in the news or advertising business in the first place; and in the second place, how did one get hired; and in the third place, how would I be able to deal with an editor? Then suddenly, in a flash, it hit me—I could be an editor. Editors, it seemed to me at the time, were essentially writers, and they most likely drew regular paychecks. Sounded like just the thing.

The problem was that, in the mid 1970s, there were no university programs that I knew of that trained editors, and many of the creative writing programs now in place, such as the one at the University of Houston, were then only seedlings. Besides, who was going to hire a young tyro with a dream of being an editor but with no experience? And where in Houston could an editor work besides the newspapers?

It all seemed hopeless, and the problem weighed on me for the next year as I finished school and went to work full time running the layout department of a print shop. The work was a logical extension of the part-time work I'd done while in high school and college, and it had the added benefit of teaching me the technology of publishing if not the techniques of editing.

During these youthful years, I had a number of literary and arts friends, and all of us were in the same boat with regard to our writing and/or art and our futures. Among them were Steven Robinson, who was a songwriter, and Lazaro Aleman, who had been writing fiction for several years. We began getting together casually to talk about writing, usually at Steve's apartment because, at the time, he was married and Lazaro and I were single. Over the next several months, these casual get-togethers became regular weekly sessions, which we dubbed Sylvie's Salon after Steve's wife.

Not long after Sylvie's Salon took on its official name, I finally realized how I could gain experience as an editor and publish not only my work and the work of my friends, but of other Houston writers and artists as well—I could start a literary magazine. I'd been working in print shops for several years, I had the understanding of the technology, and I could do it inexpensively. Also, I knew enough writers to get the thing started and, I thought, keep it going long enough to attract others I didn't know. Maybe I could encourage the literary community in Houston and, in doing so, encourage and teach myself.

I produced the first issue of *Phosphene* in the late spring of 1978 with the assistance of two friends: Jean Croce and Randall Hajovsky. It was a small-format magazine, 5.5" x 8.5", saddle stitched, with 56 pages and a press run of 500. With equal amounts of optimism and presumption, I gave it a cover price of $1.00. The content consisted of poetry, essays, fiction, humor, drawing, painting, and photography—a pattern that remained throughout *Phosphene*'s short life.

Soon after I began working on the second issue, Jean dropped out of the project, and Steve and Lazaro stepped in. The second issue appeared in late summer 1978. It retained the format of the first issue but we increased the number of pages to 100. Again we produced a press run of 500, and the cover price remained $1.00. After this issue, Randy dropped out.

By now, we were finding a few local outlets willing to stock the magazine, such as independent bookstores, boutiques, head shops, and even a couple of grocery stores. Most of these were inside Houston's 610 Loop, though as time went on, we did develop several outlets in Austin, notably Whole Foods and a couple of independent bookstores. The sales weren't great, but we knew we were hitting the right people because we began to gain more attention from local and regional writers and artists, and the submissions grew to a steady flow.

The attention prompted us to reconfigure the format for the third issue. For that issue, released in late fall 1978, the magazine's dimensions were 8.5" x 11", and the volume was perfect bound. The page count was 60 and the press run was 300. We also raised the cover price to $3.00.

Throughout this period, Steve, Lazaro, and I kept meeting weekly, but we dropped the name Sylvie's Salon because, by now, Steve was again single. We rotated the meeting location among our three homes, and each week, we invited a promising contributor to join us. One of the first was poet Kathryn Stewart McDonald, and she quickly became a regular, helping with distribution and public relations. Another regular was Bartholo Dias. In fact, we may have been the last people in

Houston to see Bartholo before he left for South America and vanished without a trace in the jungle.

The fourth issue, produced in the late winter of 1979, kept the same format, binding, page count, and price as the previous issue, but we increased the press run to an ambitious 1,000. For the fifth, and last, issue, late spring 1979, the specs remained the same as for the fourth issue.

Alas, the attention we received, though promising from a creative standpoint, did not translate into dollars, and *Phosphene* succumbed to economic malaise, as have hundreds of thousands of magazines and journals before it. Had *Phosphene* been published today, perhaps we could have kept it alive online, but in the late 1970s, personal computers were crude and just barely impinging on the public consciousness, and the Internet was a decade away from its first burgeoning. Remember, these were the days of mechanical paste-ups using sheets of type affixed to sheets of cardboard. To save money, we did our own typesetting with what was then the state-of-the-art personal word processor—an IBM Selectric typewriter, which, incidentally, cost $1,200, or about as much as a decent PC does today!

Yes, the technology was primitive, but we were proud of *Phosphene*, and I'm still proud of it despite its flaws. In preparing this collection, it dawned on me just how many of the people we published went on to do greater things in writing or the arts. I like to think that by giving them an early outlet for their efforts, we encouraged them to continue writing despite the fact that writing is one tough career, both creatively and financially. As for me, I actually became a professional writer and editor, and I drew that regular paycheck I once hoped for as a writer until I retired. And in the process, incidentally, I've learned that there are differences between being a writer and being an editor. Some, but not all, writers can edit, and some, but not all, editors can write. The chief difference between the two, though, is that, while writers might get famous, editors are certain to get headaches.

I'm not going to name the names of those people we published who have gone on to excel, but I will illustrate my point—and its sardonic reverse—with a couple of anecdotes.

The first one must be prefaced with a bit of background. A couple of years after Steve, Lazaro, and I halted *Phosphene*, we were again bitten with the publishing bug, and we produced a second magazine, *Dialog*. Details on that can be found in the foreword to *The Best of Dialog* and are not particularly pertinent to this story aside from the fact that we did publish a second literary and arts magazine. Some years after that venture also ceased, I noticed a new publication around Houston's Inner Loop, *Blonde on Blonde*, that was publishing creative writing. I submitted a few poems, mentioning that I had founded and edited *Phosphene* and *Dialog*. I received an immediate response from *Blonde on Blonde*'s editor, Jeff Troiano, who told me that a significant number of people who submitted to him had mentioned *Phosphene* and *Dialog* as important and formative publications in Houston's literary scene.

That made me feel good.

Until a short time later, when I read an interview in the newspaper with a first-time Houston novelist, who shall go unnamed. The interviewer asked the novelist if he had ever been published before, and the novelist said that, yes, he had been. Twice. Once was in an out-of-state literary journal with a known name—and he named it. The other time was in some other literary magazine, but he couldn't remember what it was. That was *Phosphene*.

That made me feel bad.

I thought, and still think, that he was prevaricating. Seldom-published writers don't just forget their few successes. Was he embarrassed by *Phosphene*? Perhaps, though it's too bad when people don't acknowledge those who have helped them. But I guess that's the way of the world, because something similar happened later. A writer who has work in this very volume wrote a letter to the *Houston Press* about poetry's heyday in Houston in the late 1970s. He mentioned a couple of writers' groups and events but nary a word about the only publications in Houston to freely give a public outlet to local creative writers. I guess *Phosphene* and *Dialog* both are fated to be either self-consciously snubbed or too-easily forgotten.

In the end, all I can do is shrug. We helped give a voice to our time, we were a part of Houston's literary development, and we left something behind no matter how obscurely it resides in history's fading memory. But I'm not quite so willing to see *Phosphene* sink into oblivion because some of the work we published should not be forgotten. It is good work, and it represents the progress of writers who have gone on to greater achievements. So, that's the reason for this collection—to showcase this work once again.

It's also the reason that, if I knew then what I know now, I probably would have kept on publishing *Phosphene*.

—Christopher Dow

Poetry

Adrienne Anne Clark

Lazy Afternoons

Lazy afternoons
when the air looms heavy
with mug.
The distant noise of busy streets
and footsteps of hurrying people
sounding solitary on the hot pavement.
Heavy air makes us gasp for more;
when we breathe it seems we breathe water.
Distant breezes blowing in, now
and then piercing the stagnant air of our
room.
Moistened brows and shining noses
reveal the temperature of our
chamber.
Minutes, as hours, drift slowly by, promoting
sleep and cooling dreams.
We sit with eyes wide open, yet unseeing
dreaming while awake.

Hearing yawns about our ears
break the sweetness of our dreams—
momentarily.

Annette Craver

Asleep at the Wheel

It's deep before
       the dark silence of the night
Where shadow lurk
       behind doors of bewilderment
Announcing the darkness
       and the coming of fear to all
Softly spoken, a breeze, whispers by
       Stopping only once to warn
a young bird in its dusk flight
       Then, passing on slowly
It flies.
       Haunting. . .
And all is silenced by its flight
As it makes its way through the glow
       draping a dark heavy curtain over all
       Saying a soft goodbye
          to the sun. . .

Judson Crews

His Heavy

Lips and a small green
leaf dangling there

                                   certainly

his mouth is perfumed
with fresh sap

your narrow cheeks
and longish chin

                                    your eyes

slanting with their heavy lids

His arms slender and buoyant

You are covering yourself
with leaves

Will he eat them
Savoring the ferment
their pungence clinging
to your damp flesh

Michael Crippen

I Barely Escaped with My Life

I doused myself with gasoline
—the first parts to burn were my eyes and hair—
and with a minute hand signal
the air and water left me.
My shirt became a zeppelin,
filled with spirit and bone,
and my teeth marched away, unheeded.
The fumes rose, and I was left to sleep.

I slept until the earth turned again.

untitled

punctuation is important in this life
pause
because it ties sentences
and schedules   break
and who knows
(really)
may even end relationships
period

Jean Croce

Reflections on Work as a "Typist"

It is as if Kafka's bureaucrats
  have multiplied in
        carbon copies and
Xerox copies to cover the
  earth with layers of
        memos, correspondence
          and alphabetical archives—
People in rows pushing
  keys, keys of adding machines,
        typing machines, keypunch machines,
          soon to be replaced by machines
Clinging to fragile
  existence in face of
        this awful reality—
Their presence that something,
  yes, something even something
        important is accomplished with
          color coded pen marks
            and form separation
So they continue fondling
  fountain pens
Their digits ticking off
  digits
Endlessly plunging into pits
  of paper clips to
        punctuate the
          madness of it all.

Karon Crow

To the Pied Piper at Thirty
19 March, 1978

Your flute is hewn of second growth
and carved by patient touch.
It attracts of itself those who smell
the hand-rubbed grain, hand-given oils;
and those who hear in its beige warm tones
the several melodies it at once sings.

Pied Piper, the sounds hang along
the seldom noticed wanderings:
the leaf, the neck of deer, the eyes of hawks
move as your aftertones.

Your dress is of the hunter as you roam,
but also the beast, who, startled
in his solitude, will break
for heavier brush and his gold-colored den.
I seek you there—not among the children;
the melody, illusive and withdrawn
to them before the sitting,
lures by indirection.

I come, rather, as the artisan of flutes:
knowing a wood; that certain place of fingers;
the lips that burn through a tempered air.
I seek the hunter and the beast within,
the hunter within the beast, and too,
the piper who would hesitate at being found.

Knowing your history, and your fond regard
for hiding, even from the artisan,

I wait without the melody for speech
to invite me in, await the calm
of a beast cornered within himself
and the sure treaty between hunter and hunter
as territories outreach.

And I am, Pied Piper, the hunter–beast
the sound engages. I, who raised my ears
along the creekbed, sought the sound
and hushed the hunger—to hear again.
I am, Pied Piper, the hunter–beast
who waits without the den.

Earl L. Dachslager

Assignment

"Tomorrow," he said, feeling like a fine soufflé, light, warm,
And done with loving care, "write for me a poem of love."
"Homework?" she wanted to know. "An assignment?" As though
To say: Am not I, my self, sufficient, words apart?
Whoever longed for the language of love past the part of flesh?

Ah, my dear, the words are only a sign meant to tell
Another way of passion's time and turn and your special spell—
My wish for your voice, some determined need of speech
As, shall we say, a small boon for some overcast afternoon,
When I shall miss the true touch and shape of you
And long then your certain words to read and hear,
Your words, only, to urge me past my up and coming fear.

Robert Dante

The Clouds Had Ribs

we crash through a few quick towns—
Bobby's full of coffee, smoking Camels
I stare at oil wells, cattle and cactus:
it's all a dream where I bomb school buses,
                    dance black boots over boulders,
see a roof ripped apart, and, shouting,
                    skitter away
          from 2-inch thick tornadoes
in a bamboo garden—
                    I whisper into the night that I
pulled the pin
and tossed that wizard flash
that killed
          Harvey Corman

from rafters I watch
the stool below my legs
                    tip over and fall
I land on my feet
and confess:
                    magic in the first degree

I walk away from the lies
those Kill-You realities—
I think somewhere Back There was
a woman who knew me and was not terrified by
          that truth

Miles Per Hour
(for Sally Richardson)

one motel room after another
the same motel bed
                           night on night
the same TV sit-coms
                           different sets, unnumbered channels
a postcard for my pocket,
as I leave, a book of matches,
                           too—
I smoke that cigarette I stubbed out
yesterday, about this time—
the maid made my bed by noon
while I was gone, again
(I think the same invisible maid
follows me, a few miles behind)—
I can't stand it
I walk to the restaurant around the corner
                           yes checkered curtains
                           yes mints by the cash register
                           yes the trucks whooshing past
                                     the rattling windows
and yes I recognize my dinner
                           before we're introduced
and I Know
                           Exactly what I'll dream tonight
while I here watch one
more day of my life disappear, swept
into the evening swirling
                           down the road.

The Price

tonight's
dreams of memory—singing ghosts fill
    my small bedroom with northern lights—
on shores of sleep, my footprints take the waves

     *   *   *

today yawns
I wake—a dark skid
the outside bright world a blast of intravenous deja vu
my left hand in the bathroom mirror
    rubs an old scar

too much memory in the present tense
    can pull anyone's mind to pieces
but tears do not clot—each night the same
     ghosts sing their names,

my younger face
    glittering in their eyes

Red Telephones
(for Butler)

a red telephone
makes every call an Emergency—

"Hello? I'll be right over. . ."
And suddenly I'm eating two pancakes
a Sunday afternoon, with friend Butler,
watching police cars
                cruise by shimmering with sun heat
over cold coffee and conversation
through a diner's pale florescent lights

We're in one hell of a hurry,
deadline coming,
under the gun
                and ready to Go

I glance at my watch from
time to time as though to check
some urgent schedule
or countdown,
even these tile-floor echoes
of my youth
remembered
                on the run

Reverse Revenge

I am afraid
he couldn't care less—
                        I pull the trigger

the bullet spins out through his skull
                        untwists a few hairs
                        spirals back into a straight line
                        picks up velocity as it goes
into the gun's muzzle—
a puff of smoke snakes in sudden time
                        back into the barrel as I
                                    unpull the trigger

I untie him
forgive him

It always works—
he'll kill himself in three days
                        and leave his kidneys to a cousin he's never seen

Secret Music
(for Ginny)

1.

I open my eyes
new-light shock

a face I recognize before I see it
                    says my name

my dream includes reality
it is Boulder Colorado
morning

embracing water
                    glass on couch-bed table
apartment sounds through open door
embracing miracle in my arms
hands under wool blankets
curtains open to brilliant hour outside
the golden dream continues
two lovers

2.

time begins again
shirts are buttoned
streets climbed
classrooms
one classroom with dancers
two dancers with poetry in their hands

one poem with the gravity of night
two dancers midway between floor and ceiling
two compasses pointing north
one poet watching two dancers with one poem in their hands
one poem with arms and legs
one poem that slowly lifts its head
one poem that steps into the sunlight
                    with a face I recognize

Traffic Overture

I

Oh Lord—for all my sins
                    hypothesized or consummated
in the name of every person I've insulted
be he bus driver, friend, or stupid cashier
for all the evils that I have done
for all the good that I have left undone
for all that, and more, much more, oh Lord
if you had wished to punish me
                    (your fiendish Humor divine)
you would have put me on a narrow road
at a very high speed
in a horrible thunderstorm
                    with a line of highballing trucks
                    stuck behind me, honking the heavens apart
and oh Lord here I am
on that road
in this storm
with those trucks coming up my ass,
                    their bright lights on,
                        Honking, Honking

Oh Lord I swish, I sway
(will I see tomorrow, ever?)

Oh Lord, Your lightning is terrible
it frightens me from my nails to my hair, and yet
                    I cannot get off this goddamn road
this road which has no apron or exit;

Here comes another ambulance. . .

II
visions of Icarus breathing bloody water
consume me, then
Amelia Erhart pressed back into her seat,
                          knuckles white, muscles weak
next, flashes of hundreds of parachutists
                          cords wrapped around their ankles
squashed flat on the earth

Oh Lord horrible, this vision of me
                          wrapped around a tree,
or crawling out of a jagged tangle
to scrawl my blood type in my own blood across the asphalt,
watching my last desperate hieroglyph
wash away under the rain, pink then gone
                          even as I fade, face-first
or being plucked, nit by nit
out of a chromium grill,
                          a shoebox of shredded cubic centimeters
                                    of my former self

Horrible, oh Horrible:
Prometheus shrieks at that eagle devouring his liver;
my own Fears with wingtips aflame
                          are tearing at my nerves—
Will this rain ever end?

III
Lord Lord Lord Honk Honk Honk
Lord Lord Lord
Honk Honk Honk
Lord Lord Lord
Honk Honk Honk Lord

J. A. DeGar

Raining

An urn pours forth,
Rain rending waters like sand on sea
Of memories and merriment
Trickling a heartful tune
Like Harpies on an awakening.
It gives of itself—
Expecting no one to hear,
Exulting the listener.

untitled

An endless excursion
The people I pass know not where these ship's sails voyage
Inbound, crucifixes shine through neon-nighted days
Black cats and mystery give the sound
Going and coming and going again
Splashing against echoed sands
And beach blue clouds outbounding in

Bartholo Dias

Cat's Paw

The radiator sighed, Cuban crackers
Kept the beat. Nursing her prey, the feline,
A cat no more than three months old
Stroked the air with her claws, rent the atmosphere
In slivers, and scattered stars in this common heaven.
What's on top is news, the events of the decade
Brought to you by the prime of time,
Most deft of ministers.
Yea, brethren, I say, forsooth, verily, amen.
What mask will you wear tonight for your intrigues?
A two-faced mask will I wear tonight for my intrigues.
It is the cat's paw, the silent shadow, the cold caress
Come in on the tenure of night's breezes,
Dispensing the comforts of finality
To my nourishers, pride of prides,
Heart of hearts, cheek of chiefs,
Bone of my marrow, and tomorrow's sauce
Of pomegranate red waste on the tide of door
Knocks and door knobs lying on hall floors.

The Mad Smile of the Half-Moon

She stood on a burning bridge and beckoned with her eyes.
Plasticized girders began to melt like gray butter,
Dripped in spurts of steam into dark water below,
Where they drifted past glass-eyed fishes that fed
On gems among the rushes a fathom down
And drifted past the jetty's end, past the pier,
Beyond the turquoise-colored water. And in the sky
A thousand arcs of light lick the hollow of the firmament
Like split instances of time passed unnoticed,
Illuminating in dim effigy the courses of mud's rise.
So we spend our time, and dream, and hope, and finally die
To complete the illusion, that others may come in our stead.
And the woman's breath was hot on my cheek.
At the touch of her fingers on the back of my hand, memories
Rose of a mountain fastness soaring high over
The reaches of desert wastes, a mountain
Of crystal white snow peaks vibrating in the cold blue air,
A colossus of the West in infant's eyes,
Eyes that roam among the flares of bridges burned
Before the consummation of crossing.

Who Gains No Wound

Who gains no wound
Makes no sound.
Who would be lost
Has wisdom found.

Bob Donachie

The Wanderer
for Rob

You are never gone long,
In the morning they'll
Look and speculate
On which direction you

Have fallen, the ways
Your feet take you
When the moon is ripe.
It could be you were

Entranced by the lack
Of promise in days,
The immutable principle
Of death by purpose,

And they may yet be
Calling you; But you
Continue as before,
Even the bones of

Your feet uncertain,
Hearing, yes, but
Not words, or emotion—
Rather the instances

In which these sounds
Are grounds for departure.

Christopher Dow

Abandoned Ruins

In the hour of our loneliness
We lie on beds of fire.
The sun sears our flesh
As red as the bloody-headed vulture
Waiting in the deadness
Of a stripped and withered
Willow in desert ruins.
Crumbling adobe blocks
Litter the clay foundations
With their shattered forms.
Once a town lived here
On the banks of this dried stream—
Willows shaded, fields flowered
Where now the baked lizard scuttles,
Where the wild and distant burro
Brazens the heated earth
In his aimless wanderings.

In the hour of our loneliness
We lie on beds of stone.
The moon hisses through empty windows,
Whispers vision to a white seduction
As bleached as the sand
On the banks of the turquoise pool,
The last of the stream
Of the life of this ruined hamlet.
Sagebrush strokes purple
Against the still pallor,

Calling for calm thought
On this verge of desert emptiness.
The breathless air
Winds the sound of legions

Of sand grating on sand,
Drowning the ruins in dry humor,
Grinding them down inevitably
To more of the same.

In the hour of our loneliness
We rise from beds of mystery
And seek the desert horizon,
Our emptiness burned, bleached,
Then ground by waves of sand
To the fine edge of here and gone.

Pencil

Put me in your hand.
Even that small
I am the brand
That feeds the fires
Of the wars of man.
I am the lave
Of the fallen fortunes
Attending that knave.
From his blank birth
To his hollow grave,
I fill each white
Space with his motion,
And in the night
He takes my form
To the outward sight.
I am all he wrought—
Greater than the wheel
For his every thought
Revolves around me.
To him I taught
A certain permanence—
A lesson that my
Own transience
Could give a voice
To his conscience.

Mechanics of the Technological Renaissance

Mechanics of the technological renaissance—
Chrome dizzily spinning sunwise.
Tamarin run wild, transplanted
Oceans, continents, to a heritage
Of celluloid, and solenoid dreams short
The circuit of cosmic indifference for all
Their worth, leaving them unceasingly cold.
Man about to take charge of man decides
His true destiny and chooses his own path.
Volumes of philosophy number thousands.

There Is a Map

There is a map
Of our love
Here on this page.
See—
The paper is torn.

City of Dreams

City of dreams
And Tyrolean power—
Some day here
Space shuttles will
Surge to the sky
On flaming vapor trails,
Push upward
Until all that's left
Is another star.
Rockets are so like
The Tower of Babel,
Bringing men together
As they reach for the heavens
In the language of science
And scattering them like stars.

Out on the prairie,
From a particular spot,
You can see
The seven skylines,
And the buildings
Rise like rockets
Of steel and mirror glass.
This is Space City,
Here on the prairie,

Though the structures' base
Belies their space shapes.

Who wants to journey
Into the void with me?
Let's take the shuttle
Bus downtown and look
At the rocket fields.
Let's go inside
And wander through
Miniature universes
Of the social cosmos.
You can walk miles
Through blocks of buildings
And never feel a breath
Of fresh air on your face.
The mirror glass
Has exposed elevators.
If you stand close
Inside the elevator glass,
You take off.
And if you stand close
Inside the mirror walls,
You're walking on air
Above the street.
If acrophobia possessed you
You'd fall right through the mirrors,
Plunge to the street below,
To be forgotten
As a breath of wind.

Jan Henson Dow

After Reading Velikovsky

"The bones of hippopotami are found
as far north as Yorkshire?"
Did they set sail, floating northward
from crocodile infested rivers
in the warm South?
Their compass somehow circling, circling
for true North.
All about them ice flows thicken
in the cold air.
Why would any living thing leave that warm tide
to find a lost pole?
Puzzles like these interest me
though the pieces do not fit.
I have traced the archipelago of myself
across the tusks of Siberian mammoth,
a terrifying scrimshaw of breast
and belly, gums, teeth and bone
flash frozen in ancient amber.
Could I trace myself, tracing myself
back through the icy glass of time
To find the hand that holds the charcoal
thus
along a single line?

Oh America! Oh Benjamin!
Found poem from D.H. Lawrence, Studies in
Classic American Literature (1923)

Oh America! Oh Benjamin!
Doctor Franklin,
snuff-colored little man.
The hour has struck!
The free mob will lynch me,
and that's my freedom.
What did the Pilgrim Fathers come for, then,
when they came so gruesomely over the black sea?

The Perfectibility of Man!
Ah heaven, what a dreary theme!
The perfectibility of the Ford Car!
I am many men.
Which of them are you going to perfect?
There are other men in me
besides this patient ass
who sits here in a tweed jacket.
Oh, but I have a strange and fugitive self
shut out and howling like a wolf.
See his red eyes in the dark?
The soul of man is a dark forest,
The Hercynian Wood that scared the Romans so,
Here am I now in tatters and scratched to ribbons.
Even the husbandman strains in dark mastery
over the unwilling earth and beast.

The Aztec is gone, and the Incas.
The Red Indian, the Esquimo, the Patagonian

are negligible numbers.
Ou' sont les neiges d'antan?
My dear, wherever they are,
they will come down again next winter,
sure as houses.
The Red Man is dead and unappeased.
Do not imagine him happy in his
Happy Hunting Ground.

Think of it.
Eve!
And birds of paradise.
And apples.
There are ghosts in the air.

Gene Fowler

Zen 21
(A suite for Space City)

Very likely the most intriguing roshi* of the 21st century was the one who never quite got around to an answer when asked his name. He was not Japanese as was traditional and expected. But then he was not American, either, as were so many of those of the late 20th century. He once said, or perhaps only thought, that he was knot—among all the spiraling lines of Genkind's** evolvings about the Planet, but this, of course, was patently nonsense, possibly an erupting of senility.

As biographers have pointed out, he did indeed have a monastery, or said (possibly only thought) he did. But nobody actually got an adequate look at it. Some said it was too dazzling to see properly; others that it was too vague; still others that parts of it refused to stabilize in a given moment, or momenta. Roshi apparently said that his or any monastery was, slowed down, mon-aster-y—or 'place of singled star.'

The biographers also have noted that Roshi's entire teaching, the phosphene of his rubbed life, existed in four thoughts. Until now, these have not been available in print or other material form. Previous attempts to print them have not produced stable counterpoised marks, but only the base 0-sum, in the older or traditional notation, 'emptiness.' We have reason to believe, however, that this time the words and syntax selected will hold sound.

* A Japanese term that translates 'master' and incorporates the sense of both 'teacher' and 'prototype' or 'exemplar.'

** An American term introduced by Kate Swift and Casey Miller to replace the patriarchal 'mankind,' referring to the transgenderal Jinn in the species bottle.

i.

'how to sit'

The single star under our
fingers is no single star, but
constellar—
five points, or six, or seven, or
bubbling laughter of
points.

Orion's belt, the Pleiades cluster
born of the eye's
dance.

The gathering spires.
the expiring reach—shoulder
blades arching
apart—

spreading ribs out from keel
and forward

to bounce back and float high

points laced
by the dance of wit's
core and eye—

the bent knee, the true thigh
rush into dark

wait ahead the star.

ii.

'how to breathe'

In the dying time
horses dance away
from mounting,
hillsides ripple
against walking,
dreams gather up storm-dark
at the horizon,
winds sing that dying time is here,
gusts howl and moan
their dark song,
and Sirens flash sun-yellow
inner thighs,
snort through flared nostrils,
and dance away
from mounting.

'Come to the dying time,' merlins
caw, 'Come
to the dying time.'

And the sea, great ball of yarns,
tangle of flawed
crystal threads running,

rises up, dancing Sirens, to flash
sun-yellow breasts

                              and dance away
and the egg, blue-white
on the palm,
minuscule atmospheres on the palm,
dreamed
of a flying thing—
grew dark—
obsidianed mirror, smoky
song intact, at the ear
threads
its way, filaments, later, in
the cavern.

iii.

'how to accept the Con'

Filaments outward into
vastness from the supernova lacing
dark points of space, or
con-
sider that a question
is not, after
all a question—
the grandiose problem will
spread, and
spread

until it is not noticed
by the eye

peering through
at its peers

(around and around you go
        trying to find the handle, or
        a corner, at least, on this smooth)
What was asked?
Or Who asked, of Whom?
Where is it dealt with?
And peering though the question
my bulging eye finds
only an old man tomorrow and
habits yesterday and
perhaps a need
to show off—

peristalsis marks eons
and beyond
the lace
only the slow winds of unmind
coil and uncoil
crystalline geometries
wink
as I rub my magic I
but shaggy coats
wave in
laughter.

iv.

'how to re-turn'

The inner
becomes the whole beyond the atmospheres,
absolute light sources
points
with no constellating lines what-
soever,
though dark lines proliferate and wait
til need,
and the outer
becomes skin taut
across cheek bones, mouth
a line ready
to expand and snip out a frag-
ment of the whole,
eyes unidentifiable
flying form-
ations, ready to cross
trajectories
like swords on occasion. And
then the Wait,
the Great
Sit
until to-and-froings sing
the dark web,
weight
telling that one
comes, and
you

will birth
another
in your own image
that was before
your birth.

Steven R. Gilbert

Still Life

We sit listening to Stravinski.
Still life in you
Now more than ever.
You are a one piece bodyscape
Reclining to the horizon
With one movement.
My eyes dance (like Petrovshka?)
A spontaneous modern ballet on you.
I marvel at how your ascending thigh
Appropriately Crescendos
And how my heart joins the
Polyrhythms!

Geraldine Greig

In the coming railroad time of this country

we take our places at separate desks
and write our respective
upkeeps and blasphemies in felt tip
and ballpoint, you
distracted by speedboats and wind in
the sails, stock
certificates, financial
alarms, me deafened
by the antediluvian din.

Saints hold desperate seminars
in the backyard, rebels
hack the door down in front,
orphans and urchins wail
through the windows.

In the old railroad
time of this country
braids, caribou, crystal
shadows of ghosts, tall
fathers thrice dead
flow through the hunching summers
to be subjects for
felt and filmmakers
shortages later when life
speaks again in
stone's throw
crow flight
calluses.

At night our wrangling books
keep their peace
and gravities balance
in the glow of the scattering galaxies;
it's no young chieftain's giving,
no vernal light and lather as you
come to me, but early
metaphors of harvest as I stroke
the russet silk of your body in its
magnate's robe and
the spokes of your speech turn the rim
of love over
and over
me down
warping tracks.

Archibald Henderson

Easier

Easier than eye-shadow
or pollen twitched into April
by careless bee's nudge
a child's belief
away at the heels of a pony

revenue slips into pocket
like husbands into houses of ill fame
autumn winds turn
leaves into the book of years

stockings near brass in a fireplace
caught on fire burn through a lifetime

Mother's cross
I believe in Santa Claus

Robbie Henson

Cracks in Eternity

Today my grandmother is dying.
Soon her wisps of hair,
      grey, thin, and stiff will go
      and the wrinkled pit of her mouth will
      bargain for no more air.

Outside it is winter. The grey face of
four o'clock stares through the window.
      On black slush—
      the cars move toward driveways,
      and supper tables. Down
      the sun is falling into night,
      always.

She gave me coffee when my parents were out,
and always gave me what she would have kept.

There is no reprieve.
The president cannot interfere.
      Her sunken tear duct eyes,
      to the hollow, defleshed taut,
      a patron of the earth will become.

Diggers are filling the grave of my Grandmother.
Diggers are filling mine.
We are born from the black.
      The light is only a spark
      jumping off the steel
      lost before it hits the ground.

And all wills become dids.
And in time, even the eye of an eagle
Could not see the fine crack in
                                eternity
That was my life.
Everything that is,
is between creation and annihilation.
Birth is a death sentence.

Flickers of light. Ripples rising in a stream,
Sucked into the current, lost in the ultimate
                                darkness.
Lost in the blind wind of time.
Larger than time.
Larger than anything we could know.
        A well that
        answers no sound
        for the dropped rock.

Today my grandmother is dying.
A bible fills the room
With its dusty smoke.
Kleenex crumpled floor.
Wrinkled skin folded into
Piles at the elbow like melted wax.
        Stooped condolences from family friends.
        "No, ma'am, I'm not married. Maybe I'll teach.
        But I make strange phantasys."

We are the furrow people.
Scratching a life in the crack between
                beginning and end.

Planting seeds, and watching them grow
                fertilized, fortified
           with do's
                      don'ts
                      dreams of eternity
                      promises
                      crying
                      laughter
Grows—until the mountains shift, the waters tear, the crack
                                            closes

and the night screams and opens its arms

Lisa Hunter

waterlilies

       i told him i liked the painting of waterlilies
at an art exhibit he took me to.
he said it was too impressionistic,
        (i didn't understand till months later
        i read a book on monet)
           so i shut up.
       i told him i liked the movie i'd seen without him.
he said the critic from the new yorker thought
it was too passé,
           so i shut up.
       i called him long-distance in southampton
to tell him i loved him.
he said he would love to talk
        but he was having a party
        and a photographer from the times was there
        to take his picture for the society page.
           so i hung up.
you can't have bad taste forever.

Samuel H. Lerner

Antes O Despues

Antes o despues
Before or after
Asking
Antes

       o

            Despues
'You got a
lotta nerve
comin' up here, whitey,
You got nerve. . .
How do you like it?
¿Antes o despues?'
Death reaches out
Asks no question, only
    Antes

       o

           Despues?

Karen Wyatt Martin

Aditya

Cradled in the curve of your look,
I know the divinity
of a handful of moist earth,
the perfection of uncarved wood,
the graceful yielding of a stalk of grass.
It is then that I often weep,
for human flesh cannot endure
too much reality.

Aditya hridayam punyam, sarva shatru bina shanam.
(When the sun is kept in the heart, all evil vanishes from life.)

In these moments,
you come to me,
carrying the sun in your hand.

Aditya hridayam punyam, sarva shatru bina shanam.

Unquestioning,
you offer me the sun
and the wisdom
of unpolished stones.
In your presence,
I know my timelessness.
Centered in my simplicity,
I gather the universe into my look.
I move with the flow of sand.

Aditya hridayam punyam, sarva shatru bina shanam.

I slept a dreamless winter sleep
until you came. The pool was clouded.
And now,
I no longer brush dead leaves
from the surface of the pool
for there are no leaves.
There is only the pool—
still,
receptive
in its meditation,
the place where the god dreams.

Aditya hridayam punyam, sarva shatru bina shanam.

Through his look, I perceive the secret of transformations.
Shiva dances
while the manifestations
rise and fall
and return to the source
and the sun perpetuates the mystery
in which we move.

Aditya hridayam punyam, sarva shatru bina shanam.

Robin McQuorquodale

Andres Segovia's Concert at Jones Hall

1

Mr. Segovia draws his fingers over the strings,
Plucks one and then, the other:
"Arrulladora, Torre Bermeja, Sevilla."
The audience.
At intermission, the ladies in twill suits and dainty hats,
Trip toward the alabaster cups for refreshments. A moon.
       Eight cups and this moon.
Girls swing their thin arms. All of them are about eighteen.
They are a delight here.
Tunes with names come flowing out at us.
The audience.
We clap our hands raw,
Stamp our foot and feet and legs, raw.
Scream and cry.
Rave.
Tear; if you will too, we rave and tear.
Impassioned tears, love and, "I see God in this."
"Tear!"
"O, I will."

2

Maestro Segovia, we have asked the stars to wink more in your
       honor—
If this was, and it is not, the fifteenth century,
We would ask the lutes to begin all over again for you.
We would ask the centuries to skip from Luys Milan, circa 1535,
To Mr. J. S. Bach (1685–1750),
Then skip to Mario Castelnuovo-Tedesco, *La Mandragola.*

Andres Segovia, we have asked the stars, and M. Castelnuovo-
        Tedesco, born in 1895,
To do more things in your honor.

3
Maestro, sit there calmly, my love;
On that low, leather stool, sit there.
It is all you have of a Steinway;
All you will ever have of it.

4
Out of a magic sack,
A golden woven pouch,
You draw a gleaming brown guitar.
You thump on its body, and
There is thunderous applause.
The animals hear it.
Raccoon brothers up from the bayou hear it.
A mouse in the costume box hears.
The animals know.
I am one of them and I know.
The usher is but a boy, and I think he knows.
This is Jones Hall.

5
Andres Segovia, tune those strings.
Play.
Radiant angels of the entablatures like what you say,
Or what you interpret of what Señor Tedesco and Señor
Albeniz say:

"One June, biting Spanish morning,
The bull, happy to be in a sunny yard, paws the sand."
Well, Maestro Segovia, we hear you.
We could never envy you to the point of hate. No.
Though, certainly, you make no mistakes.
Rest easy, then, on your stool,
All you have of a Steinway,
All you will ever have of it.
Let that hollow arrangement of thin wood,
Guitar, all you will ever have,
Peculiar resonating box,
Not violin,
Not viola de gamba,
Hardly a lute,
let it rest beloved, on your thighs,
Covered as you are with a tuxedo, soft, cashmere and black,
Rest beloved,
Or hear our applause.
The heart leaps,
Faith; the whirlpool spins.

6
Carlos Fuentes is your pen name, but Andres
Segovia is your real name.
You walk home.
Heavily, you cross the stage.
In the wings, the fluttering, whispering, "Well done."
A strong, young arm, your valet,
Relieves you of your guitar.
You go out again, enjoying the adulation,
Stamping of feet, raw,
Roaring, wings beating in the wings,

The leaping of hearts,
Eight moons, one cup; alabaster, all of it,
Translucent and not transparent.

Angel, not actress, probably muse,
Talk to me, to us.
Support an aged, music child,
Until Mario Castelnuovo-Tedesco can get to the stage wings,
Until the good spook and shadow of Castelnuovo-Tedesco can
        get there; at least,
Until the dependable escutcheon of Tedesco can succor or save
        (get there).
The bull.
He is from Andalusia, not Attica;
Jaén, not Segovia, and not Valladolid.
Admirers are in this audience.
Neither ring, blood nor sand here.
This is a stage and not an arena. No.
A concert and not a fight!
Magic sack, not flask,
Gleaming, brown.
Guitar, you are brown.

7
Señor Segovia, I don't much believe in apotheosis,
But right now, I think that I see you on a cloud,
Where, in every other concert of the year,
I have seen only an orchestra pit.
If you'll please to do another song,
I think that the angels on the architraves will croon you upward,
And the cherubs on the friezes will croon you upward,

And the seraph on the cornice wall will croon or sing to you and to us.
What can a seraph really do? Well,
This is Jones Hall, and
"The symphony ladies have done miracles."
Maestro,
Andres,
St. Pelagia's favorite child,
Francisco Tarega's good friend,
Sit there calmly, my love—
From that low, leather stool, don't think of moving.
From now on, Maestro Segovia,
Perhaps already glorified,
Neither friar, nor brother, but
Guitarist. Sit there.
An orange flame about the size of a thimble (not timbrel, Maestro)
Is hovering above your head
And above the frets of your guitar.
Maestro, all you have to do is sit there.

8
One last thing—
You are the first in your field since Tarega.
This morning,
16 February 1979, 9 o'clock,
Above the cherry laurel and the pansy's one yellow bloom,
There was, in your honor,
An eclipse of the sun which lasted about three minutes.
Though the sky was not completely altered,
There were unmistakable changes in the light.

August

These are the things that really happened;
the vacant clouds of summer.
You told me, "I like my melons in August; I like my tomatoes
vine-ripened;
tangerines, sweet, must be picked from the trees."
Then you stepped on my rows.
I welcomed you.
I called you the fox. (You smiled like the dog.)
I watered the dahlias and the cyclamen;
Dampened us too with affection and a little juice.
Then you stepped on my perfectly aligned furrows.
This is my complaint:
You gave me your hands, wet as they were in blackberries pulled
off to the bowl.
You stained my blouse and spoiled dear-image.
(I welcomed you.)
This is my complaint:
Pretending to tie my sash, you untied my sash.
When you smiled like the dog, I couldn't get mad.

Homecoming I
to Malcolm

Breaking up the playpen, we swam the bayous;
Injected with needles,
Head and shoulders with yaupon, tender and just walking,
We were part of an important army of pines!

Under your arm, you squeezed stubs of air tickets and squeezed
          new air tickets.
Weren't we born here to leave cities?
Forget "l'oeil de boeuf" and "guirlandes de fleurs".

I pass judgment like the hare passes the holes in the corn cobs,
And the field mouse passes the pile of beer cans,
And the otter passes—although we haven't got one, and I
          haven't seen one;
Neither, honey, have we got the beaver from Gascony nor the
          swan from
Malmaison—
Heavy sighs are in unison with bayberry blowing.
Whimpering is characteristic of many of our birds.
Out of season, the stag enters many clearings.

Put down your Remington 500, place it across my knees.
Come with me to the Big Thicket.
Usually, we let the copperhead go.
We believe that he bites only when threatened,
        the unbooted foot, or
        the putrid hand.
Symbol: I offer you my fresh hand as a symbol;

Pious now, I ask you to come with me into East Texas.
Come with me to the Big Thicket.

The rumor of the pines is not the sound of the Autoroute of
          the West.
"But I hear the rumor in the pines."
"You are hearing the Dallas Highway."
"Highway 45?"
"Uh-huh"
"Is this the Partia Mia?"
"Uh-huh"

We fall kissing the needles,
Flat on the needles,
Kissing the needles, the pines;
Embracing the needles, we kiss the needles—
We kiss the ones that are nearest to us and the ones that are
          farthest from us.
We can't speak.
"What did you say?"
"This is homecoming."

Rose II

Rose, you make yourself
known between poplar trees. You
support light changing to dark; dark
changing to river and sloping lawn.
Rose, you change to fat,
lift your hands from Night's backbone,
go off quickly,
remembering who you are, and who he is.

Rose, you ease yourself through the Chisos Mountains;
rising, uprising, breathing in and out:
last summer, last year and 1958,
where the Rio Grande and the Pecos meet,
you pulled yourself to the bank,
told me how it was with
one elbow on the air mattress
and half my chin in the flat of an evening.

Royce

I

Even the daisies were tropical in 1944
And the sun-plant's open curtain,
Fanned loosely the palm tree, blue, by the cloud's blue door to
      the sea,
Forcing the tassels back and fastening them to a two-spoked
      ceiling fan.
It happened on Drexel and Tuam,
Two great streets of Houston.
The aviators broke the records,
Pushed flakes of Glenn Miller into howls of alto saxophone,
Then withdrew with their girls to the watch towers for the
      ghostly conning towers.
The next day, they went on to decorate the dance floors on
      Courtland Place,
And the art galleries on Audubon Place.
The hero, young Royce was there,
Standing in front of, "Blue Cloud and Sunset".
I was there in a robe of ticking and feathers,
Just one of the peacocks racing across the lawn,
Beauty without eyelids,
Who finally rested her head on the strings of this one man's
      bathing suit.

II

Royce,
> hug me here
> lean on my shoulder
> come to my house

It's the Fourth of July

From my lawn on Shadow Lawn, you can watch the fireworks
> which are going off under Sam Houston's horse;

With this rifle and this telescopic lens, you can shoot out the
> streetlights on Main and on Fannin.

Royce, I think the world of you, always have.

I would whisper this even in the mouthpiece of a public
> telephone:

Weren't you the one with the gun?

Yesterday, I saw you crying,

Your head was on the bar in a bar on the corner of Crawford
> Street and Avenue C;

Weren't you the one with the gun on the shores of Tripoli?

** ##

My address is 36 Shadow Lawn.

** ##

From my lawn on Shadow Lawn

** ##

Under the acacia trees.

James McCracken

History Lesson

Simply
chaos, everything
canceled out,
thousands of velocities
thrive—
placid
the eye
turned,
sliced the first form.

The Peril of Travel

Back
from such a distance
to the same
dissonant chair,
to this precarious desk
between Scylla and Charybdis,
with the littered pyre
of selves in books
and clumsy scratchings of experience.
I begin the pruning:
underneath,
ashes.

Pat McCulloch

Do Dead Men Walk Down Dowling Street?

Rosie Greer for Pabst Blue Ribbon beer smiles
a 300 pound grin
 in niggertown
past Green's Almeda
 Bar-B-Q and
Frenchy's Po-Boy
Black sax and not
5th Avenue and no
Neiman-Marcus either
for that matter 'cause
money don't talk on
 this side of town

 It whispers and screams
Do Dead Men Walk Down
        Dowling Street?
    You tell me
when you see the blue
cars with the bubble
machines cruise
down niggertown looking for bullet-ridden
ghosts of Fred Hampton.

Martha McDavid

I wish you had been higher. . .

You said you'd be a bass guitar
and I said why
when maybe you could have twelve strings
eight more places to be touched,
or the lead, a front line stance
carrying the major strain

but you said No I'll take the back
four strings to remember
and stay low key in this performance
watching you pick
other players.

Passage

Deliver us
us of the rift between
closet and podium
our old blushes now on stage

Deliver us
whose mothers did
through safer channels
than our own, so questioning

Deliver us
from every father
eager boys to make us mothers
demanding us as little girls

Deliver us
to grow again
unimpeded by the blood
our awesome fertile reckoning

destined to repeat ourselves
as we plunge forth, overripe
so long waiting to be opened
sometimes splitting, unredeemed.

Two Forces

I want to lick your grin
begin
a shocking love affair
shuck the space between us
climb in your underwear

I want to take you like a Tristram
through a waterfall and fuck
in dark green moss
in water
up against a tree for luck

Don't think I couldn't love you
or that I do, or would
but remember that I chose you
you were standing
and I heard your blood

beating. From a room away
I saw the white specks in your eyes
clear a passage for me
so adept
so unwise

I raped you as I shook your hand
I knew that you would understand.

Kathryn Stewart McDonald

Always

Sitting on a bench
As even stars die slowly
Certain only the sunrise.

Early morning clouds
Hide river willows bending
Dew moistened trees cry.

Limitless echoes
From fear never far away
Sorrow has icy fingers.

Explanation

The black hole of the universe
An exit
Through which emptiness is
Expelled
Once realization sparks awareness
Of lost humanity
Far too late to make amends with
Mankind
The silent screams of suffering are seen
As exploding suns
In distant galaxies traveling eternally outward
To the edge of nothing
And then beyond the void the epitome
Of isolation
Colors never canvassed rage in those shades of dark
All things must end unseen as sons are born
Until suns die
And even the remains of suns are sometimes seen
But too late to touch
From the edge of here and now to
Somewhere else
We send our metal monsters for clues
Searching
Unceasing curiosity
The end results from ignorance.

For Franz and Photographs Left Behind

With camera nailed like night
To nullify only the emptiness
Eyes so narrow could not see

Records made realizing remembrances
Of reality from which so far
Removed and remote he grew

Scavenger of solace he sought
Scenes of sempiternal sorrow
Savior now of shattered and scarred

Finally the forage from which
He forestalled his defeat from
Feeling and forejudgement faded

Left after capturing cautious remnants
Of characters possessed by carnaged catechisms
Careful lest his camera be revealed

My friend, death is dirty and deceitful
Drugged and drowned you died
As all your dreams were left demeaned

For the Whale

Death dancers
From the sea
Came this raj
To die

On sacred sands
Of Nan Madol
Dance your mourning
For the king

He lies wearied
Ancient warrior
Proudly scarred
Taboo for feasting

Shaman sing
Tale of Tears
Song of Sorrow
Honor these bones

Magnificent modengi
Raj of the sea
We weep for you
We weep for you

Safe at last
From Ivory Thief
Safe at last
On sacred sand

Masks for Lost Faces

At the edge of the world
Someone sang a song to God
The ultimate audience of one
A song of sorrow and mistakes
With a dance from a broken dream
Counting scars with steps
Left the world, became instead
Sacrosanct and certain
So judgments failed and then
Sheltered from society

Now with a mask for everyone
Something strange and unseen remains
And reflects only those faces now
Who buy and sell a name
And with the broken dance
Steps sing words unsaid, thus
Nothing is lost in translation
Plaster cast or sculpted mask
Icicle melting fast
The last fly of winter—an albino roach

Or a butterfly in the snow, even a
Broken rainbow in a midnight onyx sky
An impression of that face might show
What really is or who was.
As even plaster masks cannot
Conceal or deny the eyes
Magritte is gone
None are left to fear
As no one really looks
Behind the eyes.

Saipan

Saipan you sleep surrounded by sea
Gentle your jungles, soft in the light
My home, my home, crying, calling to me

Saipan you sleep surrounded by sea
Washed warm by waves lost from my nights
Mystical music makes kind memories

My home, my home, crying, calling to me
Magical mountain now far from my sight
Island of emeralds remember me

Saipan you sleep surrounded by sea
Hear me shaman, nothing here that is right
Totem of Taga please set me free

My home, my home, crying, calling to me
Return my soul, sky spirit, lost light
Taga, protect me, so far from the sea

Saipan you sleep surrounded by sea
Totem of Taga please set me free
Island of emeralds, I remember the sea
My home, my home, crying, calling for me.

Shades of Stillness

A shoreline free from storm
Traces wet shadows
Quiet clouds and solitude

Three unbroken turtle eggs
And driftwood
Damp sand at dawn

Sidi Bou Saiid, Tunisia

The moon on turquoise Tunisian nights
Gleams ghostly on the minaret of ivory mosques
Sirocco sand does not blow in spring

Light fog feathers the land
Curls itself and wraps around
A gnarled olive tree

God sleeps in the street
Still warm from the last day's sun
Night shadows are long and thin

This desert never fights
It dances to the shores of Carthage
And colors the world gold

Sidi Bou Saiid on the back mountain
Has risen from the sea
In blue and white jasmine perfection

View from a Cliff

Centuries of fog
Gently shield the sea
From the glare of stars

And fishermen
Glide through the night
With lanterns.

Robert McGough

Bob Early's Grocery Store in Arkansas

In front, the grocery basket is full
of watermelons. There are only four.

On this day the bicycles stand
unchained to the posts they lean on.

The thermometer assures the street,
"Dr Pepper Hot or Cold,"

while the new Coke machine waits
for the day it too will be

like the screen door:
old, dented

and used to children's hands.
Fat Bob Early looks out late

today, remembering
the watermelons in the heat.

The afternoon lies on the ground
in small

patches.
He puffs outside

and looks past the watermelons;
what is thrilling is his son's red bike.

Sidling past the basket, he looks—
yes, the street is quiet as it sounds—

hoists himself onto the thin bike,
a watermelon on wheels

likely to fall and break open
until the bike's shuddering fit passes

and the wheels straighten.
Past front windows packed with neighbors

Fat Bob Early rides, laughing
first from fear and then speed,

out of the town
into Arkansas

Harryette Mullen

Easter Colors
for Easter Pittman, who pieced the quilt

would it be safe to wash this quilt?

it smells like an old lady's attic
but it is so beautiful
even dirty

the colors are joining hands and dancing
a pattern repeating itself

it reminds me of Busby Berkeley musicals
the geometric dances
k a l e i d o s c o p i n g colors
squares   triangle   diamond   and stars

circles
the patterns
your greatgramma made
pieced-together colors from clothes
handed down
and down again
till no one else could wear them
a pattern repeating itself

tonight we add to attic memories
wrapped in the warmth of this quilt
the new/old smell of our sleep

old clothes odors
smells of beds and bodies
they the music the colors be dancing to
the patterns repeating

would it be safe to wash this quilt?

B. Parker

untitled

Lucky day, spring night
Sound of Southern boys
Goin' no place special.

Dim at first
Headlights brighten
      gather momentum
      shoot across the ceiling.
They fade.
I'm still here
Remembering how the shapes felt.

It is important
What you remember
Or is it how you remember?
Who can tell?
Might be relative,
Might be absolute.
Mostly it's space
With energy in between.

Looking for patterns
In a new medium—
      figures on a page.
Must I apologize if
      they are not nude?

Your lines are too short
Chopped down, essence of.
Excuse me, but are you writing poems?

Why? Ya'll poets?

Hell no.
We just like short lines
Hit home, unafraid.
But apologize just the same.

I might say hello
or
Silver tongue of the West

Somewhere the sound of soft dare
Tearing corners off placemats.
Gentle men, I accept.

Marsha Lee Recknagel

A Friend

Inseparable, they called us,
and we were.
Through school we were like
eccentric actresses,
flighty,
our moods found no mediums
only extremes
like all young girls changing,
confused,
like a snake must be seeing his old
skin lying lifeless
next to him.

We grew together so long
we finally grew apart.
I, going off to school,
You, going crazy.
Your letters to me,
strange ranting.
The familiar squiggly writing
by some unknown hand
guiding what once was Jane.
Lives no longer rhyming,
awkward in our new roles.

I was busy trying to
untangle us.
You confident in your insanity,
me, unsure of mine.
They wrote me long letters

explaining you to me.
Locked you up, a part of me,
in a cold white hospital.
I cried for both of us.
Because I knew
you were only laughing.

Oklahoma

You seemed so harsh
in your freshness,
smelling of cornflakes,
sweet hay drying in fields.
Basking in a flood of sunshine
I wilted.
Dust got into my life,
Between my teeth, in my eyes,
Settling into a film of silt
on the top of my water glass.
You seemed so young, in a hurry,
Mocking me for my slow manner, soft drawl.
I was a stranger among cowboys
wearing shiny boots, red kerchiefs
lassoing long hairs Saturday nights.
Your Indians, not tall, proud,
like Geronimo on a Cheerio box
but stumpy, with pimples and squinting eyes.
You were to be my escape
from the cobweb world of large white houses
nigger maids.
I traveled your boundaries
But found that you were only a state
Not a visa to happiness.
So I left you.
Now I'm still searching,
Journeying within different borders,
Wandering, still restless, within myself.

Steven Robinson

Blue Star Mission of Hope
(A song)

Well my name is Buster Graham,
And I ride the Southern rails
I'm making my way to the west,
But I stopped to say hello, to
Some people that I know.
And to get just a few hours' rest.

Well I'm fifty-five years old, and I
Wear a purple heart, did my
Part in the Second World War.
Scratched my name on the back
So to tell it from the rest,
But it won't bring too much anymore.

Refrain:
Where did you go, Blue Star Mission
Of Hope, I hear they tore you down
A month ago. I'll always remember
The shining blue star
Where the lost and the lonely would go.

There's a hole in the street
Where the mission used to stand,
Where they offered us soup and bread,
And I think about those times, cause
We shared our beaten souls, but by
Now them old men must be dead.

Ragged men sit and talk, of their
Children and their wives, some are proud
And some others don't care, and they can't
Remember how things got twisted all around,
Too much whiskey and too many years.

Refrain:
Where did you go, Blue Star Mission
Of Hope, I hear they tore you down
A month ago. I'll always remember
The shining blue star
Where the lost and the lonely would go.

untitled

Where in the world are we now
Our hearts are empty and so are our bellies
We have no decisions to take no provisions to make
We watched their demise in a holocaust wake

We long for the taste of the sun
And the touch of a sound

When does the soul cease its sleep
And waking return to the dream of its willing
No truth for the sake of a lie if its souls
Are to fly,
Releasing an image ascending the sky.
The joy is the best of the pain
To lose is to gain.

Barbara Winder

The Problem of Wild Horses

"Many wild horses are small, scrawny, and often undernourished. . . . Yet, these wild horses are increasing at an astonishing rate."—Dr. Walt Conley

Wild horses graze under a ripening
moon up country in Carson Forest.
Unlike tame horses who lie down
in stalls, they will sleep
all night under the stars,
tails giving an occasional
flip against flies.
It's good they don't know
how old they are, or that
winter is always coming, or
that somewhere there are bins
of grain and bales of hay.

Wild horsed gallop on the dry
river-bed. Red flags quiver
in their nostrils when they run.
They don't know to be ashamed
of their washboard ribs.

At night if I close my eyes
tame mares and geldings go through
their paces shining and predictable.
So I lie with my eyes open, hoping
to see the watering-hole where
wild horses drink. If I am lucky,
some night I might even lie
beside them, sucking the good water
between my teeth.

Christopher Woods

Shadow
(for Frederick)

new orleans, French maiden and madam
i am mesmerized by your lethargic pace.
geriatric streetcars straggle the rails
and tatters hymns of southern lace
only to whisper to themselves over brick avenues.
i wake, at different times,
to find this all
deaf and dumb and maybe damning,
artifacts in the river of years,
victim to an urban renewal of a spirit.

wrought iron rusting, the delta steaming,
the senility of slave smiles launching away in the past,
we sit in the autumn of the century
considering juleps that were.
we were.
and by the hooting echoing dawn
browsing the whitewashed cemeteries,
your lips tasted marblesque,
strong as market coffee.
the ambivalence of shopworn lives
sheds in the high and mighty creole noon,
when the all of us are uncovered of ourselves
and the mardi gras mask.
the only prayer in an absinthe haze
is that the fog never lifts entirely.

much the same as riverboats that to and fro
we straggle on, rising like a new race out of the South,
in scents of wisteria from a jasmine past,
plodding along a course that asks
an end to all the short-lived dreams
rising from the dust.

John Zern

untitled

We're all fixin to go dancin.
We're all gonna go too fast.
Tonight we're all gonna go to the race track.
I'm gonna go where y'all go.
Deep in it all.
The summer daze
is here again, just like in '74.
The music is on.
I'm in my trance.
It's hot. I'm behind tinted glass and conditioned air.
It's strange. I'm strange.
Oh God, I look strange in my sun glasses.
That unnatural angularity that makes everyone look twice.
I like that.
That look and that look.
Is that the look these days?

Fiction

Lazaro Aleman

Colorado '71

THE HITCHHIKER SMELLED EARTHY, OF wet hay or crushed grass. He was young, bearded, and wore a sheathed knife strapped to his leg.

For a long time after he got in the car, no one spoke.

The gentleman driving was in his sixties. He and his wife were vacationing up in the mountains for the summer. Now, they were going down to the valley for their weekly groceries.

The gentleman watched the hitchhiker in the rearview mirror. He regretted ever having picked him up. In fact, if he had seen the knife earlier, he would never have stopped. He didn't know what had gotten into him.

The knife made him very uneasy, and he began to drive faster. The sooner I get rid of this character, the better I'll feel, he thought.

"You might take it easy around these curves," cautioned the hitchhiker. "There are a lot of hair-pin turns around here."

"See, Harold. It's not just me."

"Hush, Bertha. Young man, I have been driving forty years now. I think I know what I'm doing."

"It wouldn't hurt to slow down," said his wife.

"People go over these cliffs all the time," said the hitchhiker.

Just as he finished saying this, a hair-pin turn came up.

The old man had to apply the brakes and maneuver very quickly to avoid going over the side. And even then, the two right wheels skidded the shoulder of the road. The hitchhiker sat forward and grabbed the back of the lady's seat.

"See, Harold!" she screamed.

The old man was forced to slow down. He had both hands clenched tightly around the steering wheel and his palms were sweating. But the more he thought of the knife, the harder his foot pressed down on the gas pedal.

"Are you folks from around here?" asked the hitchhiker. He had decided conversation might slow the old man down.

"Oh, no! We're from Kansas," said the wife. "My husband and I are vacationing up at Brainard Lake. We have our trailer up there."

Keep talking, thought the old man. He'll get all the information he needs, and tonight he'll come back with his friends.

He tried giving his wife a warning look, but the road demanded all his concentration. So instead, he settled for a "hem, hem."

His wife did not hear him, or if she did, she completely ignored the sound.

"Do you live around here?" she asked the hitchhiker.

"Peace Valley," he said.

"Is that like a hippie commune?"

"Not exactly; we . . . ah, sir, there's another sharp curve coming up. . . ."

"I saw the sign."

The old man slowed the car to a reasonable speed. Far below, they could see their road and the cloud-shaded peaks of the surrounding lower mountains. The hitchhiker sat back in the seat and refused to look down again.

"I swear, I dread these drives into Boulder," said the nice lady. "Harold drives like a madman sometimes. I don't know what gets into him."

"I want to get back up before dark," he said.

"It takes us only an hour to do the groceries."

"Still," protested the husband.

I'll kill her when we're alone, he thought. I will literally kill her.

"Why don't you buy your groceries at Ward?" the hitchhiker suggested.

"Ward?"

"It's a little town near where you're camped. They have a grocery store and a cafe. You could probably buy most of what you need there."

"Hear that, Harold? We have seen the sign. It says Ward Cafe and has a dirt road winding down the side of the mountain. But Harold figured it was an abandoned mining town, and so we haven't stopped.

"It was," said the hitchhiker. "But the young people have built it up again."

"Hmm. Is that where you live?"

"No, ma'am. I live at Peace Valley."

"That's right. Is that very far?"

"About three miles into the woods from the road where you picked me up."

"And you walked that whole distance?"

"It's nothing. I walk it every day."

"'Nothing' he says. I walk a block and get winded."

"That's lack of exercise," said the hitchhiker. "People have become too dependent on the car."

"You sound just like my grandson," said the woman. "As a matter of fact, you look a little bit like him—except for the beard and long hair. Doesn't he look like Jimmy, Harold?"

The old man looked back in the rearview mirror.

Looks more like a tuft of tumble weed to me, he thought.

"Yes, a little," he said.

They had been climbing and descending, mostly climbing while they were conversing, and now the final descent began. They rounded a shoulder in the mountains and far below appeared their road and a deep blue lake cupped in the mountains. They went around another curve and the lake disappeared.

The old man rode his brakes the whole way down. Still, the car kept gaining momentum and screeching around the curves. There was already a very strong odor of burned rubber.

Then, suddenly, the road leveled off and the lake reappeared, much larger, with a small town in front of it that the peaks had hidden earlier. In the late afternoon sunlight, all the buildings appeared to glow with an inner light.

"That's Nederland up ahead," said the hitchhiker. "I'll be getting off there."

"You're not going on into Boulder?" asked the old man.

"No, I'll go another day into Boulder. They're probably having a heat wave down there anyway."

"Oh."

Coming into the small valley, the temperature had already changed considerably; it was much warmer.

The old man drove slowly through the rural outskirts. Nederland was a typical mountain community, with the majority of houses all bunched in the center and the rest of the town scattered sparsely all over the surrounding hills.

"You could probably do your groceries right here," said the hitchhiker.

"Oh no. No, we'll go on into Boulder," said the old man.

In the center of the town it was warm and dusty. The houses were all old and dirty looking. A wind blew and started a dust cloud down one of the dirt side streets.

Civilization again, thought the old man.

He eased the car off the road and stopped in front of the Nederland Post Office. Like all government agencies, it was the sturdiest building in town.

"This is fine," said the hitchhiker. "Thank you."

"Nice meeting you," said the old lady.

"Yeah. See you around."

The elderly couple drove off very slowly now.

Damn fool, thought the hitchhiker. It's drivers like him that make me almost want to get a car sometimes.

II

The young couple stopped at the Ward Cafe on their way across the mountains. They had been trying to make Estes Park and the Rocky Mountain National Park before the end of the day. But the way their VW was running, they were lucky to make it this far up.

"You go inside and order something to eat," said the young man. "I'll put gas in the car."

"I'll wait," said the girl.

There were two relic pumps standing outside the grocery store half of the building. But no one seemed to be attending them. James honked his car horn.

A young boy stepped out of the grocery store. He looked about twelve, carried a small knife, and wore his hair in a ponytail.

"Yeah?"

"Two dollars regular, please."

The boy wound the old pump handle and inserted the nozzle in the tank. Then he leaned back against the car and watched the faded numbers skipping past.

"Tell me," said James. "Do you know how many more miles it is to Estes Park?"

The boy shrugged.

"You'll have to ask inside," he said. "I just mind the pumps."

James paid the boy the two dollars. Then he backed up the car and parked it across the street from the cafe. Below him now, he could see the town of Ward, scattered all down the mountain slope. It was a very derelict-looking town.

He locked the car doors and joined his wife on the steps of the cafe.

Inside, the cafe was quite large. It looked like something out of a western movie. There were animal heads and miner's tools all over the walls. There were also large photographs of the town when it had been a mining community. The photographs were old and faded, but the town looked about the same.

James and his wife went and sat at the long counter opposite a huge wall mirror. On the mirror before them, they could see the front picture window and their car and the mountains beyond.

Behind them were the dining tables, arranged in a circle in the center of the room. The tables were all covered with checkered cloths, and each had a jar with wild flowers in it. There were the booths set along the right wall, with a door and steps leading down into the grocery store half of the building. The kitchen was off to the left in a separate room.

A few longhairs were sitting at the counter, drinking beer. A young couple occupied one of the booths.

The waiter came over now. He was a long-haired, bearded freak, too.

"What will it be?" he asked.

"Do you have pies?"

"Fresh homemade pies untouched by sterile machines," recited the waiter.

"What kind?" asked the girl.

The waiter went to the glass cabinet and checked. He shooed a fly away.

"Blueberry and cherry, right now," he said.

"Blueberry," said the girl.

"Cherry," said James. "And two large Cokes."

"Would you like ice cream on the pies?"

"No, plain," said James.

"I'll have vanilla on mine," said the girl.

The waiter cut large chunks out of both pies and lay a large scoop of vanilla ice cream on the girl's dish. Then he replaced the pies back in the cabinet and brought the two plates over. He set forks and two Coke bottles before them.

"Is that all?" he asked.

"For now," said James.

The waiter threw a dishcloth over his shoulder and walked to the end of the counter. There he started a conversation with another long-hair.

"What do you think of this place?" asked James.

"Scary, but I like it. And you?"

"Definitely. It has charm."

"Maybe we can stay here."

"You mean that?"

"Why not? We both like it. Besides, we already saw the rest of the country once. This is new."

"I don't know. . . ."

"Remember, 'he who hesitates is lost.'"

"I'll ask the waiter," said James.

They finished their pies and drank the ice-cold Coca-Colas slowly, enjoying the taste. It had been a long time since they had enjoyed a cold soda. James called the waiter over.

"Was everything all right?" he asked.

"Great. We were wondering, are there many places for rent here?"

"Here, none." The waiter smiled. "You're the tenth person today to ask me that question. No, there's no places for rent. Everything is taken up. But you might try Nederland or Gold Hill."

"No, we like it here," said James.

"How about campgrounds?" asked the girl.

The waiter scratched his head. "Well, there's the canyon, about six miles down. Or there's Brainard Lake. . . ."

"How far's that?"

"Three miles up."

"Is there snow there?" asked the girl.

"Hey, Rusty. Is there still snow up in the Brainard Lake area?"

"More than you'll like," said Rusty.

"Good, we want to see snow," said the girl.

The guy named Rusty walked over now. He had hair the color of rust. He was also tall, heavy, and wore a lumberman jacket and patched jeans with a sheathed knife strapped to his right leg.

"You people going up to Brainard?" he asked.

"It looks that way," said James.

"Mine if I come along?"

"No, come."

"Far out."

James paid the waiter. On the way out, they passed an elderly couple coming into the restaurant.

"Hello, again," said Rusty.

"Hello," said the nice lady.

Outside it was already early evening, crisp, and it looked like a storm was forming. They got into the car and started up the dirt road leading to Highway 119. The hitchhiker gave the directions. He pulled out the knife from its sheath and began cleaning his fingernails.

"How's this Brainard Lake?" asked James.

"Like really far out, you know."

"How about fishing?"

"Fine, if you're into that. But you need a license there. Like where I live, it's really far out. There's this lake right behind my cabin and I just fish right off the porch. Like the other day I caught some really far out rainbow and speckled trouts."

"Where's that?" asked James.

"Peace Valley."

They were climbing up a very steep grade now and the VW engine was straining in second gear. James's ears kept popping and unpopping.

"You people want to turn on?" asked the hitchhiker.

"Sure," said James.

The hitchhiker pulled out a marijuana cigarette from behind his ear. He lit the joint and passed it on to the girl.

"This is home-grown stuff," he said. "We call it Boulder Bad."

The grass was a florescent green color. And it scorched the throat going down.

"I can see why it's called Boulder Bad," said James, coughing.

"It takes ten to really get you off," said the hitchhiker. "Then you get a headache for the rest of the day."

They drove past Red Lake now. It was off to the left through the trees and there were a few mobile campers parked along the north shore of the lake. Then they rounded a curve and the forest closed in behind them again. The temperature was dropping steadily. Through the trees in the distance they could see the snow-crowned peaks of the true Rockies.

"This is beautiful country," said the girl.

"You think this is beautiful, you should see the western slopes," said the hitchhiker.

"Where's that?" asked James.

It sounded like a town to him.

"Well, we're on the eastern slopes now. So, if you were to take a car and drive over the mountains, the western slopes would be on the other side of the mountains."

James looked back in the rearview mirror. The hitchhiker looked perfectly serious.

One of us definitely has been affected by the grass, thought James.

They finished smoking the first joint and the hitchhiker lit a second one. Then by the time they were half-smoked with the second one, Brainard Lake came up.

"I'll get off here," said the hitchhiker. "I have some friends to see. You can camp anywhere along here. Have a good time."

"Thanks for the grass."

The hitchhiker made a face.

"Here's another one for later."

He handed them a joint and started down the cinder road toward the lake.

"There's some really beautiful people here," said James.

"Yeah, but he smells funny," said the girl.

III

"See, Harold. They all wear knives here."

"I still don't like it," said Harold.

The elderly couple was sitting at the Ward Cafe, enjoying a late snack. The room was crowded with young people now. Outside, it was raining.

The waitress came over. She was very young and wore a floor-length dress with hiking boots. Her hair was pinned back in an old-fashioned bun.

"Would you like anything else?" she asked.

"No, thank you. I don't even think I can finish this pie. Who did you say made it?" asked the lady.

"Dale's the cook, but we all helped," said the young waitress.

"It's very good," said the lady.

"Thank you."

The young waitress smiled and walked over to another table.

"She wasn't even wearing a bra," said the old man.

"Oh, Harold. It's the times."

Two young men walked into the restaurant now. They were both covered from head to foot with dust and both carried knives on their hips. One had a thick black beard. They sat at a table opposite the elderly couple and the young waitress walked over.

"How's the prospecting going?" she asked.

"We dug a lot of dust," said the bearded one.

"Maybe tomorrow," said the girl.

"Yeah, tomorrow we're going farther up into the mountains. We figure we'll be gone a couple of weeks."

"I wish I could go," said the young waitress.

"We'll take you when we find gold," said the younger miner.

The old man got up.

"I'm going to get some cigarettes," he said. "Finish up."

He walked across the worn wooden floor and through the door, down the three steps to the grocery store. It was a very limited store. Only the essentials.

There were three long-haired youths drinking beer by the entrance, watching the drizzle outside.

At the cash register stood another young girl dressed similarly to the waitress. She was talking with a girl who was buying a loaf of bread.

". . . that's how they raped her," the cashier was saying.

The old man edged nearer, pretending to study the cigarette display.

"But couldn't she run away or something?" asked the girl customer.

"Run away? There were fifteen guys. They tied her up and beat her and made her do all sorts of things. She says they told her if she didn't cooperate, they would kill her."

"Christ, that happened here?"

"Just a few miles down the road. It's a motorcycle gang. They've been camped in the canyon for some time now. Anyway, some of the guys in town are planning a meeting for tomorrow night to get together and run them out."

"I hope they do. Christ, I use that road everyday. But how did the girl get away?"

"One of the guys took pity on her and untied her. He told her to get the hell out fast and not to even look back. So she hiked up the canyon and across the forest for three days. When she got here she was all bruised and bloody; hadn't eaten in five days. But she's all right now."

"And I've given rides to hitchhikers along that road," said the girl customer, shaking her head.

"That's how they got her," said the cashier. "Only she was doing the thumbing. Those guys are crazies. Excuse me . . . yes, sir?"

The old man was standing right in front of the cash register now, listening. He had quite given up his pretension of studying the cigarette display.

"Oh, ah, a pack of Camels, please."

The girl searched her display case and came up with the correct brand. The old man paid her and went back up the steps to the cafe. His wife was still sitting, sipping coffee.

"Still, Bertha?" he asked.

"Sit down, please."

The old man objected, but he sat down anyway. It was already getting gray outside and he wanted to be on his way. He hated driving at night, especially in the mountains with the roads wet.

"Watch that kid over there," said the old lady. "Every time someone leaves, he walks over and eats their leftovers. He must be starving, poor thing."

"They're hard kids, Bertha. Very hard."

The old man watched the leftover kid a little while.

"We better be going," he said, finally.

"All right, but leave a nice tip."

The old man left a quarter tip. And the old lady left half her blueberry pie on her plate. They walked out the door hand-in-hand.

All the way up to the camp, the old man was silent. It was obvious he had something on his mind.

When they arrived at their trailer, he went inside and lit their Coleman lantern. It was cold in the trailer, but the heat from the lantern soon warmed the little room. They sat in the cubicle kitchen and stared at the dusk outside. Already, a few campers had their fires going. A cold wind was blowing hard off the lake.

Then it was night. The blackness closed in around the little trailer and opaqued everything.

"Listen to that wind," said the old man.

"It reminds you of Kansas, doesn't it?" she said.

"Yes, it does."

There was something strange in the old man's voice. For a long while, neither spoke again.

"I've been thinking," he said finally. "Perhaps we should leave. I don't think we belong here."

"Oh, Harold."

"No, Bertha. You were right. I think I understand that now. These are hard kids; they have to be. Remember the first time we came to the mountains?"

"Remember! You were twenty-five and I was nineteen."

"That was thirty-eight years ago."

"Our honeymoon," she said.

"Those were good times, the '30s."

"Very good times, Harold," she agreed. "But why talk about it?"

The old man's eyes were shiny.

"We were hard then, too, Bertha."

"Yes, Harold."

"We should never have left here; or leaving, we should never have returned," he said.

The wife looked at him, but said nothing.

"Trying to go back to anything, once the ripeness is past is . . . no good."

He tried to say it nice, but it came out clumsy sounding. It was an old truth he had relearned now too late in life, and he wanted, needed, to share it. But the right words would not come.

"We'll leave tomorrow, all right?" he said instead.

She nodded.

"Maybe we can even go down to Florida," he said. "We've never been there before. Leave the mountains . . . for a while."

The old lady took his hand and held it. She knew it took a lot for her husband to say what he had said. And it tore her inside to hear him say it.

"I didn't want to tell you," she said, "but the cold has been aggravating my rheumatism."

"We better go to bed," said the old man. "We've got a lot of traveling to do tomorrow."

He picked up the lantern and lighted their way into the bedroom. Outside, the branches from the blue spruce trees rubbed against the sides of the trailer and the wind whistled shrilly.

The old man turned off the Coleman lantern and lit a cigarette. Then he climbed under the blankets and smoked quietly. The old lady was soon asleep.

But for a long time, after the light had ceased, the old man lay awake and remembered.

IV

In the warmth of their fire, the young couple sat and smoked the marijuana cigarette the hitchhiker had given them earlier. The fire crackled and shadows danced on the trunks of the surrounding trees.

"It's a beautiful fire," said the girl.

"Yes, it is. I'm glad we collected that wood before the rain," said James.

"Yeah."

In the road, someone was walking toward the lake. They could only see a black shape and hear the clopety-clop-clop of the stranger's boots on the cinder road. They heard him a long time after the figure disappeared.

"Looks like our senior citizens have retired for the night," said James.

"Kind of early, isn't it?"

"You know how it is when you get to be that age; you need all the beauty sleep you can get."

"That wasn't very nice."

"No, it wasn't. I'm sorry."

James leaned forward and fed another log into the fire. The wind was blowing hard, flattening the flames.

"Did you see them?" asked the girl.

"Yeah, they drove up in their huge Lincoln Continental and got into their nice comfortable trailer."

"You sound jealous."

"No, not really. More sympathetic. They're missing so much."

"Maybe they're too old to rough it," she said.

"Then let them go to some hotel on Miami Beach."

"My, aren't we hard tonight," she said.

"It's the grass." He laughed.

The smoke from the fire shifted around suddenly and blew into James's face. It made his eyes tear. But he refused to move, and, finally, the smoke shifted again.

"I'm glad we found this place," he said.

"Maybe we can move here . . . for good," she said. "I'm sure we can find exactly what we want down in Ward, if we wait long enough."

"You mean that? About staying?"

"Why not?"

The wind gusted through the trees and almost put out their fire. Then it was silent and cold and black, and the fire made the only sounds.

"We better get to bed if we're going mountain climbing tomorrow," said the young man.

"I hope we see snow."

"We will, even if we have to climb the highest peak."

The girl took the flashlight and went inside the tent. James stayed behind and checked the tent stakes to make sure they were secured. Then he urinated on the fire, kicked some dirt over it, and went inside, too.

The girl was already in the sleeping bag.

"I hope this wind doesn't blow the tent down," he said.

"If it does, we'll really be cozy then," she said.

James stripped down to his underwear. "Damn, it's cold!"

"Hurry in. I'll keep you warm," said the girl.

V

Suddenly, the monster came to the hitchhiker again. Lying on the hard cot, listening to the wind outside, the monster stole silently upon him.

He finished the cigarette he was smoking and stamped the butt out. Then he rested his head back on the cot and stared at the ceiling.

Outside, the wind was blowing hard and cold. He could hear the lake's water breaking on the shore. The wind came in gusts, but the waves broke steadily. It was the waves he liked to listen to.

It's going to be another cold night, he thought. Tonight and tomorrow. Why is it I can't get used to this cold? California was never like this. California. Ah, yes, California.

He was beginning to get the old urge to travel again. The monster was definitely stirring within him tonight.

Colorado's becoming too crowded, he thought. Too many new people coming in. Too many tourists. Too many younger freaks. Married freaks.

The land was losing its charm. Even Ward was becoming too established. Motorcycle gangs. Police committees. When he had first come, the people were different. They were hard people then. Real people. But most had left now. In fact, he was one of the few still remaining from the original crowd. And now the trend followers were coming in; they were spoiling the land.

Time to travel, he decided. I've already outgrown this place. Colorado is definitely spoiled.

But there were other places. He had heard some fine things about New Mexico and Arizona. In fact, some of his friends had headed that way. That's where he would head. He needed a change of scene.

Tomorrow, early. He would start out for New Mexico or Arizona. He didn't have much to pack.

Now he closed his eyes and rested peacefully. The monster was in complete control, and it would keep through the night.

(1972)

Letting Go

IT CAME OVER HIM IN a rush—this overpowering urge to travel. He was speeding home on the turnpike, thinking nothing in particular, seeing nothing in fact, the highway one mechanical routine, when suddenly the monster seized him.

Sure, why shouldn't he go on the road again, he thought. He had the money. College was over, for the summer at least. And he was free, wasn't he?

Anyway, he was tired of fighting his natural impulses all the time. This feeling had not come over him in a long while. He had feared having lost it forever. And now that it was back, he didn't want to risk losing it again.

Maybe he was ripe for the road. Maybe the monster sensed this, and it had returned to lead him. Certainly it came much stronger, much surer of itself.

And even if he couldn't follow through with it, he could pretend and run with it for a ways, couldn't he?

That was the problem, though. He had pretended for too long now. He had teased the monster within him. He had raced alongside of it, giving it rope, making it believe it was truly free, letting it carry him almost to the very brink, and then at the last moment always snapping the leash, bringing the monster to heel.

Maybe that had driven the monster away from him. Maybe he had abused it too often, tiring it. He didn't want to abuse the monster within him again, ever. But he was afraid if he chased after it this time, he would not be able to make the final jump.

Yet, even as he thought this, he realized something that completely jolted him from his thoughts. He wasn't heading in the direction of his apartment any longer. Where the turnpike divided and he normally went right, he veered left, toward his parents' house. But why? The mere thought of visiting his parents set his heart racing and the blood throbbing to his ears.

Yet he did nothing to change the direction of the car.

It was as if he had suddenly lost control over his body, or something stronger now commanded him. He could relax in the seat and enjoy the scenery; the car would drive itself and deposit him in front of his parents' house. At least, it felt that way.

James watched the road. It was late morning, and traffic was minimal except for a few commercial trucks and late stragglers. These looked like tiny black boxes in the shiny distance. And the sky, a crystal dome, glowed electric blue with icebergs of white cumulus clouds drifting low on the horizon.

It was all too beautiful. A perfect day for leaving. The type of weather one could ramble forever under without ever getting bored. It reminded him of other days and other highways. Other times. He imagined all great explorations had begun on days like this.

The thoughts set ripples of excitement pulsating throughout him. He might actually go on the road again. Might, could . . . damn, he would!

Still, fear washed at his resolution. Underneath the surface optimism lurked the suspicion that he would back down at the crucial point. That was always a possibility. Then deep down inside, so deep he could barely fathom it, sat the conviction that this time would be different. It was something hard and cold and small like a shiny pebble at the bottom of his stomach. Something special and excitingly new.

At Palm Drive, he exited off the turnpike and made a left turn towards his parents' house. He would race the monster almost to the very brink, and then he would see what would happen. Maybe the momentum would carry him across.

One thing remained certain—he had never before let the monster run this wild and free since his first trip. Perhaps that indicated something.

Now at the corner laundromat, he felt his grip tighten around the steering wheel, and his whole body tensed. But he did not hesitate. He turned the corner, and his foot actually fed the gas.

He must be crazy, coming this close!

Fear overtook him at last like a huge tidal wave and submerged him. It tumbled the monster from his grasp and drowned James in its paralyzing fluid. Then it rolled on, leaving him bitter and nauseated with himself.

Enough, he thought.

But his body would not respond. His foot still fed the gas and his hands guided the steering wheel, against his better judgment, or what had emerged as his better judgment. It was as if he had truly lost control over his body or something weak within him were struggling for control. He could feel the two emotions battling simultaneously inside him, and all the while, the car crept forward the last block.

Then something snapped and something else relaxed, and a certain calm fell over him.

James focused his eyes straight ahead on the road and blanked his mind. He was vaguely aware of sunlight skipping overhead through the branches of the trees that canopied the little street. That and motion. Then he felt the car turn the last corner, and all motion ceased. A deafening quietness settled over him. He didn't remember turning the steering wheel or stepping on the brakes. He was only aware of the oppressiveness of the heat and the silence around him.

The hard something inside him had fizzled and died. He could feel the hollow it had left behind. It was as if the monster, after having dragged him the last block, had momentarily collapsed and gone to sleep.

Still, something of the original impulse lingered. Something pushed him on.

He opened the car door, hesitated, and then proceeded up the cement walkway to the front door. Another moment's panic, and he knocked hard on the door. There was no answer. James knocked again, harder. Something gone within him, he began to take life again.

I tried, he thought.

But even as he thought this, he started around the side of the house toward the backyard. It was as if his legs had gained a mind of their own, and they were following their own whims now. James had nothing to say about it. He only hoped that the rest of his self would follow accordingly.

His father was standing out on the back patio, toying with a fishing rod. He seemed both surprised and pleased to see James. Then the initial pleasure gave way to a half-conscious scowl.

"What are you doing here?" he asked, cordially as possible.

"Just driving past," said James. "I thought I'd stop by and see if there was anyone home."

His voice sounded strange and far away to him now. Maybe it was the lie that made his voice sound strange. But the lie was out before he could even think it.

"Don't you have school today?" the father asked.

"School's over for the summer. Matter of fact, that's where I'm coming from. I just took my last exam. This morning."

"How do you think you did?"

"All right, I guess."

"Guess!" The father looked up questioningly. "Don't you know?"

"No, not yet."

James moved around his father to the side of the patio table and stood in the breezy shade of the huge beach umbrella. Then he pulled a lawn chair from under the table and sat down. He could not bring himself to mention the trip. It was the foremost thing on his mind, and he wanted more than anything else to say it quickly and get rid of it. But the mere thought of confronting his father with it, actually saying it, stampeded his heart and set the blood rushing to his head so fast that he feared blacking out, and so he stifled the thought.

Still, the urgency remained. And the urgency coupled with his inactivity combined to produce an acidity that ate away at his comfort and his very peace of mind. It was a slow, agonizing pain nowhere in particular but everywhere, and it burned and drove him mad with anxiety.

"I'm surprised to find you home," he said finally to relieve the torment when the silence promised to continue.

"Today's my day off. Wednesdays."

The manner in which his father said this offended James, and he immediately withdrew back into himself. Anger replaced fear and mingled with self pity to create hate. He was sorry he had ever come. Why did he always put himself in such positions? He wished instead that he had kept going when he had felt the urge. Now he had lost the monster again, abused it.

No, he had to do it. It wasn't too late yet. He hadn't come this far to turn back. It had become a test now, a challenge.

"Have a beer," the father offered.

"It's too early for me just yet. . . ."

"I'll have one," said his father. "Mind getting it for me? Inside the fridge. You know my cup."

James got up and went quietly into the house, glad to get away.

The kitchen was dim and quiet, spookily familiar with its locked-in odor of ripening bananas and other fruits. But it also looked much smaller and old fashioned than when he had inhabited it. Twelve months hadn't changed the place, and yet it had. The house already seemed alien to him. Something about it frightened him. It was too narrow, too confining.

"There's Cokes in the fridge, if you prefer that," James's father called from outside.

"No thanks," said James.

He opened the beer bottle and poured its contents into a battered tin mug that he had given his father one Christmas long ago. It baffled James why his father still insisted on using the worn mug as his drinking cup. Then recalling that early Christmas awoke in him other happy times together that he wanted to erase now.

James threw away the empty bottle and hurried out.

His father sighed. He had rested the fishing rod against the wall of the house and was seating himself on the cement steps outside the utility room. He looked exhausted. The perspiration rushed down his bare chest and rolled over his basketball beer belly and onto the patio floor.

James tried not to notice the gray hairs or the corrugated wrinkles under his father's eyes. It always made him sad to see his father growing old. Somehow, he felt responsible.

"Well, did you get it fixed, or is it worse now?" he tried joking.

"It'll do," said his father, very serious. "It had a little quirk when I cast out, but I think I fixed it."

"That's good," said James.

He looked at the fishing rod and the crooked shadow it made against the wall and nodded to himself. Then there seemed nothing else left to say, and feeling his father's eyes on him, he looked away. He wished now he had a beer to keep his hands occupied.

He hated these long pauses in their conversations. It seemed he should be used to them by now, but he could never get used to them. They always made him feel self-conscious and awkward. He wanted their conversations to run smoothly. Instead, they stumbled along.

James began to perspire. He watched the shadows hard-edge across the patio floor as the sun broke out from behind a flock of clouds. Then the sun hid again, and a soft breeze stirred the nearby trees.

"So, what are you going to do now?" the father asked, placing his mug down.

"I don't know," said James. "Probably nothing. . . ."

The father nodded slowly. He studied James a few seconds longer, looked down finally, then picked up his drinking mug again and took another sip. It was obvious he disapproved.

"I might . . . it's hard. . . ."

It was no use trying to say it, thought James. The words just stuck to his throat. And he felt his stomach knot and pull taut.

"Are you going fishing today?" he asked for conversation's sake.

"We were going to. Robert was supposed to pass by and pick me up about an hour ago. I don't know what's keeping him, though." The father checked his watch automatically.

"Are you going out on a boat?"

"Nah, just out to the bridges."

James nodded. "It's a good day for fishing," he said.

"If it doesn't rain."

"I don't think it will."

"Those clouds eastward look like rain clouds," said his father.

James squinted up at the clouds. They did not look like rain clouds to him, but he did not want to argue. Conversation was just beginning to go good, and he wanted it to continue. But already, it had stopped. He looked down at his hands and studied the sky some more.

Robert would be coming any minute now. He could feel it, and it made him angry that he would not have time to work up to things. So why did he always have to work up to things? Why couldn't he just tell his father straight out?

James stretched his legs and yawned. Then he sat upright again and looked around the yard once more, avoiding his father's eyes. Always avoiding his father's eyes.

Suddenly he jumped up.

"Let's go have a beer at the bar," he said.

"There's beers in the fridge."

"But the bar's has better atmosphere."

The father shrugged. "All right."

"I'll even treat," said James.

And suddenly he felt very silly. What had ever prompted him to suggest a bar. And what did his father care for atmosphere. The whole thing was too fabricated. It was too unnatural. Surely his father saw through it all. It embarrassed James to think that he was being so obvious.

His father finished his beer and set the empty mug down gently on the patio table.

"Let me go inside and put a shirt on," he said.

"I'll wait in the car," said James.

He had a half-baked notion to start the engine and leave. Leave and forget the whole crazy thing. Why go through this hell? It wasn't worth it.

But sitting behind the steering wheel, waiting, away from his father, watching the sunlit little street, the pine trees swaying back and forth in the breeze, he felt confident again. First far away and so weak he could barely recognize the feeling, then much closer but still faintly, the monster stirred within him. It was all the encouragement James needed.

His father walked out presently, wearing a clean work shirt and a different pair of slacks.

"All right, let's go," he said, climbing into the front seat.

"What about if Robert comes?"

"My car is home. He'll know enough to wait . . . if he even comes."

"You direct me to a good bar, then," said James.

"There's no such thing as a good bar," said his father. "Just drive down to Palm Drive and make a left. There's one right across the street."

James started the engine, went to gun it, then remembering, eased it into first and crept forward to the corner. He made a complete stop, checked both ways, signaled, and maneuvered a perfect left turn. He drove very cautiously now, the way his father had taught him many years before. It was important that he do everything right.

"Do you transport dogs and cats in this car?" his father asked.

"What. . . ?"

James looked toward his father, who gestured to the seat. Right where he sat there was a huge rip in the seat cover, and the cotton tripe gutted out of the seat.

"Oh, that." James tried smiling. "Yeah, I'm going to have to reupholster them," he said.

"You would do better to get another car," said his father.

James nodded and looked straight ahead. Yeah, sure. But there were other things that were more important than ripped seats and cars. Things his father did not seem to understand. Things. . . .

James's inadequacy to voice his feelings out loud further enraged him.

He began to think of his father sitting next to him, grading him. That was what it amounted to; his father graded him, and he performed for his father. It had been that way ever since he could remember. But why did he still play up to his father's expectations? He wasn't a kid anymore. It was getting to be a very bad habit.

At the corner of Palm Drive and Fourteenth, James came to a rolling stop, glanced both ways casually, and gunned it across the street. He screeched into the parking lot of Ye Old Keg Bar and turned the ignition off. His father said nothing.

Inside, the bar was dim and cold. There were only two other men that James could distinguish, and they were standing at the far end of the room, under a bare light bulb, playing billiards.

His father chose stools near the entrance. There was a lit juke box behind them and a tiny window to their right. The window had been painted black. Sunlight glared through the cracks in the paint and made tiny silver worms. The barmaid was nowhere in sight.

James was glad for the darkness. He already felt silly about what he had done outside, and he didn't want to have to look at his father. He was always embarrassed by such outbursts afterwards. Now he sat and watched the two billiard players. It took his mind away from his embarrassment, and besides, he loved the way the multicolored balls exploded and collided one against the other across the green felt table. He loved the bright enameled colors and the way the two men played.

"Want to shoot some pool?" he asked.

His father looked at him funny.

"I didn't know you played billiards."

"Not too well. But I play."

"We'll see," said his father.

The barmaid came over now and began wiping the counter with a red checkered cloth. She turned the cloth this way and that, and all the while she chewed gum like a big lazy cow. She had a very huge bosom, and her make-up was very heavy, but there was still something interesting about her face. She looked like she had been a beautiful woman once.

"Yes?"

"Two Budweisers, please," said James's father.

"Will that be all?"

"For now."

The barmaid nodded, picked up her cloth and walked away. She looked very bored. James watched the way she moved and he liked something about her movement. But he disliked her attitude.

If you're so bored with your job, quit it, but don't make us suffer your misery, he felt like telling her. Then he remembered his own case and the anger ebbed away.

The barmaid returned with two frosty mugs and set them on felt pads on the hardwood counter. His father would not let James pay.

"But it was my invitation," said James.

"Later. This one's on me."

He handed the barmaid two dollars.

"Keep the difference," he said.

James took a long quaff of his beer and relished the first icy draught. The beer was deliciously cold, chilled to his stomach. He took another sip and rested the heavy mug down slowly, glancing around the room. The two billiard players were setting up a new game.

He turned back to his drink and took another sip. He knew exactly what he wanted to say already. It was all nicely packed and rehearsed in his head. Now it was just a matter of letting it slip out.

He took another quick sip of his beer and tightened his grip around the mug. Then another sip and he was no longer enjoying the taste as much. He was drinking for drunkenness now.

How stupid it all was to think he could really do it.

He watched the effervescent bubbles rocketing to the top, forming a suds head. He would sit here, drink a few beers, talk a lot of rot, and then go away without ever having mentioned a word about the trip. That was exactly what would happen. What always happened.

"Why did you bring me here?" his father asked. "What's the problem?"

"Problem?"

"I'm sure you didn't bring me here just to share a beer and play some billiards."

"No, not exactly. But what's wrong with it? It's something we've never done before. I just thought we should put an end to this war. . . ."

James looked down at the beer mug, embarrassed. He hadn't meant to say so much. It had just come out.

"All right." His father smiled, little-boy-like, embarrassed by his own interest yet anxious for the rest.

"It's nothing, really," said James, hesitant. There remained a strained quality to his voice, like it was being filtered. He stared at his drink and his father waited, watching him. It was a very penetrating stare.

"I'm thinking of leaving Miami . . . going out west."

There. It was out. Finally.

"Permanently?" his father asked.

"I don't know. Maybe."

His father turned back to his beer and pursed his lips. He took a slow sip of his beer. He had expected different; prepared for worse. But this was bad enough. He could not think of anything to say.

James felt the silence tightening around him, choking him. This wasn't anything like he had anticipated. He wasn't prepared for this. But silence could be just as deadly. What was that line from *Macbeth*—"to turn back now would be as tedious as to go on." Something like that. He decided to continue.

"I want to go out west . . . to Houston maybe. I hear the jobs are plentiful there and the living cost is lower. Cliff moved there with his wife, and they're pretty satisfied with it. I don't know. I might not even like it there, but I have to try. . . ."

James looked up for the first time, staring at his father straight in the face. His father's eyes shone slightly moist. But he managed to smile.

"If that's what you've decided, why tell me?"

He no longer spoke as a father, or if he did, James no longer heard him as one. Instead, he saw a little old man, stripped of all familiarity. His father was a stranger sitting next to him. James saw how vulnerable the little man really was. And the transformation touched him.

"I'm telling you because you have a right to know," he exploded.

Something inside him gave way. It was like a bottle that had lain corked and frozen somewhere for a long time and someone had finally popped the cork, or a pent up stream that had finally broken its barrier.

"I know how you and Mom feel about my leaving," he said, choking on the words. "Mom especially. It isn't easy, I know. Being an only child is rough both ways. I can even understand now that it isn't easy for the parents either. It's taken me a lot of pain to understand that. . . ."

At first, the words trickled out thin and jerkily, squeezed almost. But now they were beginning to gain speed and intensity, flowing freely, smoothly. It surprised James how easily they flowed.

"I don't want to hurt anyone anymore," he said. "And I don't want you two to think I'm forgetting you. I know that's one of your greatest fears, being abandoned in your old age. But if one is going to forget someone, you can do it living in the same city. And there's always the telephone, and letters. . . ."

James paused. He had much more to say, twenty-one years' worth, and his head swirled with words. But his father had stopped looking at him. He was staring into his beer mug instead, solemnly, as if he expected to find salvation there. It dismayed James to think he had been speaking for nothing.

"Well, what do you say?" he asked, a little perturbed.

His father smiled weakly. He rolled the mug between his huge callused palms, raised his eyebrows, and shrugged.

"It's hard," he said finally. "It's a very hard thing for us to accept."

James felt the dam within him closing again, tightening around his throat, choking him. He resented his father's self pity act, or what he considered his father's self pity act. But he forced the channel open again.

"I know its hard," he said forcibly. "It's hard for me, too. I've been turning this thing over in my mind for months now. It's been eating me up. I'm tired of not sleeping nights thinking about it. That's why I came to you. I can't carry it inside me any longer."

"It's hard, all right," agreed his father. He took a long sip of his beer, sighed, and set the sweaty mug down gently.

"It would be selfish for us to want you to stay here, especially when your career beckons you elsewhere. . . ."

James said nothing. Now that his father had finally opened up a little, he wanted him to empty out, too. There was too much stored up hostility between them. Too much silence. But his father didn't say anything else.

James decided to wait and make sure. He swallowed the last swig of his beer and felt a tiny rush to his head. It was the slightest titillation, a minute swelling sensation, but he knew from experience that the beer had already affected him.

"How do you think Mom will react?" he asked.

"You know your mother," said his father.

James nodded. How well he knew his mother. He had tried not to even think about her so far. Thinking of her would have only spoiled everything. In fact, he had forcibly rejected the subject from his mind until now.

Somehow, he wasn't as frightened of the topic anymore. It needed to be discussed. Demanded to be discussed. And it surprised him how willingly he had brought it up himself.

"I'll tell her if you like," his father offered. "I'll prepare her for it at least."

"No, I'll tell her myself," said James.

It was something he had to do alone. Something he actually looked forward to doing. Something he had avoided too long.

There would be a scene, naturally. His mother would cry and carry on like it was the end of the world. Or maybe not. He could never really tell with his mother. She might take it as well as his father had. That was a surprise in itself. Who knew? Maybe his mother wouldn't cry. He would certainly prefer it tearless. But if the tears came, he would be ready, too.

Then there would definitely be that last goodbye scene with the whole family. He would like to skip that one for sure. But he knew he couldn't. He would just have to face it and then it would be past. Everything passed.

Sure, it would be unpleasant. But there were a lot more unpleasant things in life. Might as well get used to it now. Life was unpleasant from the moment you realized you were going to die until the day you died except for a few pleasantries along the way, and in time, even these turned sour sometimes. He knew that much from experience. But a man to be a man or stay a man had to learn to take it. Being a man wasn't a simple end. It was a means to an end, the most important end—living.

James felt very philosophical. Beer always made him introspective. He wanted to share these new insights, but he knew his father would disagree.

It didn't really matter, though, because he felt very close to his father suddenly. Closer than he had felt in a long time. Then, he had never spoken so honestly with his father before. It was all a matter of communication, or the lack of it. For the first time in a long while, he could view his father as a fellow man rather than a threat. And there were things he wanted to say to this new friend that he had hoarded too long.

The beer had begun to wear off. He felt flushed by it, but the initial high was gone.

"You know, we've been fighting each other for so long now and have accomplished absolutely nothing but hurting each other. I think it's time we forget our differences and become friends. Friends can have differences and still respect each other."

It sounded corny, but he didn't care. He felt what he said.

"That's all I ever wanted," said his father. Then, rather abruptly, he added, "What about your college?"

"College?" It caught James off guard. "Well, if I get a good job, I won't need to finish college. Otherwise, I can always finish my degree elsewhere. I really don't know yet. But it's something that will have to wait."

His father nodded, not exactly pleased, not condoning the decision, but merely nodding like a man who has no other choice. He was remembering another boy saying something similar to his father many years before. That had been a mistake, he realized now, coming to the city. A country boy had no business in the city. The city was hard enough on those born in it, let alone outsiders. But once a boy became a man he had to make such mistakes. It was the price of knowledge, mistake making. And James had certainly come of age.

James's father nodded to himself, thinking. Maybe he had been too hard on James. Maybe he had tried too hard. He had tried not to make the same mistakes his own father had made with him, but maybe he had erred in the opposite direction, over-protecting James.

It was hard bringing up an only child. It was the worst mistake he and his wife had made, having only one child. But then, it hadn't really been a matter of choice. The doctor had told them another child would kill her. Maybe they should have adopted a child, though.

So many doubts now. He knew they expected too much of James. When you had only one child, you did that; you put all your dreams and hopes into that one chance. It made it hard indeed, both ways. But you really couldn't blame anyone, though; it was just the way things happened.

He had known for a long time this day would come. He understood James was running away from them as much as he was running toward anything. It was his way of establishing his independence. But it was too late to do anything about it now.

He wished he hadn't been so strict. He wished he had been a better friend. So much he understood now. But understanding didn't take away from the pain. And it was painful, losing James.

He smiled to himself, ironically. Funny, he had waited so long for this moment—to be sitting in a bar with his son, sharing a beer—but now that the moment was here, it was not exactly the way he pictured it. Things seldom came the way you wanted them though; he was old enough to know that. At least, there were speaking again. Be thankful for that, he told himself.

Who knew? James might not even like Houston. Sure, that was always a possibility. The traveling fever might be a passing thing. There was always Cindy. He had forgotten about Cindy! He had not seen her in a while. But James would never leave her behind for long. They had been going together too long. Unless . . . maybe they were getting married!

Suddenly he felt very light-hearted himself. There was no sense to make a rainstorm over a glass of water, as his old man always used to say.

"Miss," he called. "Two fresh beers."

He picked up his mug and drained the remainder of his beer in two easy gulps. It had become an important moment for him and he wanted to celebrate it the only way he knew best—with a fresh beer. But to the barmaid, the occasion meant nothing. She came over very bored looking and refilled both their mugs then left without even waiting to collect the money.

Her attitude was very antagonistic. James took a sip of his new beer and savored its coldness then looked around the room. The two billiard players had gone. Now would be a good time to suggest a game of billiards, he thought. But he didn't feel much like playing anymore. He noticed that a couple occupied one of the booths along the wall. He hadn't seen them come in. Or maybe they had been there the whole time and he hadn't noticed them. They were a very merry couple. In the ensuing silence, the woman's shrill voice became very dominant.

"What about Cindy?" his father asked suddenly.

"She's fine."

"Is she going with you, or. . . ?" He couldn't say the rest.

"Neither," said James. "That's all finished."

He saw the shocked expression which crossed his father's face and he wished a million times he could have spared his father that hurt. He knew how fond his father was of Cindy, and his dream of grandchildren. But he would have found out eventually. It was better that it was out now. He couldn't lie anymore, even if lying made matters easier.

But he hoped his father would not ask him further questions. Embarrassing questions. Cindy and he were finished. But it was still a fresh wound. And he did not want to make it bleed again.

His father understood. Anyway, he didn't ask anything. Suddenly, the happy mood which had alighted on him flew as quickly. He nodded into his beer, and the subject was closed. Everything seemed closed. The beer drained out of him and left him weak and hollow inside. There remained only one question left to ask. And he wasn't sure he could ask it.

"When are you leaving?" he asked finally.

"As soon as possible. Friday morning if I can manage."

James's father nodded. He started to say something else then changed his mind and said nothing. There seemed nothing left to say. He glanced at his watch, feigned surprise, and downed the remaining beer in three hard gulps.

"I'd better get back," he said. "Robert should be there."

"Yeah, I got a lot of packing to do myself," said James.

He had dreaded this final moment, and now that it fell upon him, he didn't know how he would behave. Goodbyes always gave him a lump in his throat. Besides, things were going so good now he didn't want them to end. It seemed they had just started talking. There were still so many things he wanted to say. Things he would never find the time or the courage to say again. And other things stored so deep within him he could never bring them up again, not even to himself; not now at least. And maybe never. He had only skimmed the surface.

Still, the relief was monumental. He had gotten out the most important thing. And it gave him a drained out, empty type of feeling, pleasant but not as completely satisfying as he had expected. He didn't feel ecstatic or anywhere near it. A little high, maybe, but not ecstatic as he had expected. It was all very anticlimactic. And all the while, he could feel the little high leaving him.

James guzzled down the remaining beer to bring back some of the high. But the beer only made him feel bloated.

His father had already paid the barmaid. He sat waiting for James. Now he dropped a fifty-cent piece on the counter and they both walked outside into the blinding light. It was like stepping into an open oven. The heat blasted them and penetrated through their clothes to their chilled skins, warming them. It felt pleasant after sitting in the icy bar so long. They stood there on the blazing sidewalk and let the sun sift into their very bones, baking them.

"Do you want a ride home?" James asked.

"Nah, I'll walk. It's only a few blocks. You will pass by the house before you leave?"

"What do you think?"

James's attempt at old-time kidding fell flat. His heart wasn't in it, no more than his father had meant what he had asked. They were only words now to fill the time, to postpone the inevitable. And the heat hung over them like a blanket, smothering them.

"Be careful driving home," his father cautioned. "You've had two beers already."

Before James could reply, his father turned and started away very fast. A few feet further he waved his hand behind him in a goodbye gesture without ever looking back. Then he ran across the street, gained the other sidewalk, and continued with his urgent pace.

James watched until his father had disappeared around the laundromat. Then he climbed into his car and started the engine. He backed the car very fast into the street and gunned it out.

Seeing his father hurrying away like that had ruined something within him. It had spoiled the last grain of triumph.

No doubt, his father had done it on purpose. He couldn't help resenting his father and yet he couldn't help pitying him at the same time. He was especially angry at himself, but why he didn't know. And the high had completely worn away now.

It already seemed like days since he had first felt the monster and he was afraid it would not come back to him. He didn't want to think he had lost the monster. He didn't want to remember his father hurrying away that way, either. Especially, he didn't want any more scenes.

Maybe he hadn't done the right thing. Maybe the trip to Texas wasn't such a good idea. What would he do in Texas? It still wasn't too late to cancel his plans. No, there was still plenty of time for that. That thought relaxed him.

Then the thought of a strange city and old friends began to excite him. In any case, there was the trip. For a few days, at least, he would be traveling on the open roads again. Maybe he could even extend the trip a little; take a little swing into Mexico. There was a thought, Mexico! Who knew? He might decide not to stay in Houston after all. He might decide to come back.

That was always a possibility.

James felt the monster stir within him. It came from a great distance away, a minute tingling sensation in his stomach, crawling up his spine, gaining speed and intensity, rising, rising—

It rushed upon James and swept him along again.

Sure. There was always the possibility that he might not stay in Texas.

That was always a possibility, now.

Mañana

THE SUN WAS JUST RISING like a red balloon in the melting gray of morning when Tomas Sanchez parked his old car in front of the factory. As usual, he was the first one to arrive. He went directly into the locker room and changed into his khaki uniform.

It was 6:30 a.m. by his wrist watch, and the parking lot was still deserted when he went outside. He lit a cigarette and sat down on the cement steps to wait for the bell to ring.

The sun climbed slowly. Then the other men began arriving one by one with their unkempt Monday faces. They grunted hellos at each other and disappeared into the dimly lit locker room.

Tomas listened to their conversation. He answered sometimes, smiled other times, smoked another cigarette, and watched the sky come up ash-blue over the pea-green canal.

So far, the morning had been routine, but he knew that this was to be the last such morning, and that made it different. Tomorrow was the day of his promotion to foreman; that made this morning special.

The first bell rang. Tomas jumped up and dropped the cigarette stub from his leathery lips. He stepped on the smoldering butt and fell into line smiling cheerfully; it was going to be a fine day.

The solemn line of khaki filed silently into the dim building and flooded around the huge sleeping machinery, the men's feet stirring up the ancient dust into golden icicles of sunshine. The men formed in separate little puddles around the steel monsters and waited for the second bell to ring, talking quietly.

Then the bell rang and the workers scattered in all directions. They pushed green buttons. Angry red lights flashed. Amber lights winked. Motors whined. And the still machines grunted and yawned and came to life, humming like a swarm of angry bees, their tireless steel jaws opening and closing hungrily.

Tomas looked on and smiled. I am lucky, he thought. Tomorrow I will be foreman of the welding department. Me,

Tomas Alexandro Sanchez, a foreman with my own air-conditioned office. Margarita will be happy now.

The thought tickled him. Tomas laughed. He put on his suede gloves, a leather apron, dark sun goggles, and the dented yellow helmet with the glass face guard. He loved that old helmet. He was really going to miss it. He cradled the welding gun in his huge hands and shook his head softly, remembering all six years they has spent together.

"Good morning, Tomas. I understand this is the last day you'll be welding for us, eh?" The head supervisor winked. He spoke in an unusually friendly manner.

Tomas nodded. "I think so, Mr. White."

The supervisor smiled and extended a thin freckled hand.

"Congratulations," he said.

Tomas nodded, and his bronze face blushed. "Thank you, sir."

The supervisor threw his arm around him. "Hey, no more of that sir business," he said. "Call me Jim, all right?"

Tomas looked down at his scarred shoes and nodded, childlike. When he raised his head again, his eyes were shiny. "Okay—Jim," he said.

The supervisor smiled. Then he began thumbing through a collection of pink slips he had been holding in his hands. He glanced down at a plastic-coated sheet and pulled out three of the slips. "Here," he said. "You'll be doing this yourself pretty soon. These are today's orders." He handed Tomas the three slips.

Tomas studied them for a second, zealously. The he took his helmet off and scratched the back of his head. He placed the helmet back on and smiled. "Eh, what about yesterday's unfinished order?" he asked.

The supervisor frowned. "Forget it," he said. "That can wait. We gotta get these out first, by tomorrow at the latest. They gave me hell upstairs today again. They say we're getting too lax down here. Production is falling short. You know what that means."

Tomas nodded. "I understand," he said.

"Good," said the supervisor. He turned around and signaled an overhead crane with his hand. Seconds passed, and the giant crane remained stationary, oblivious to the command.

"Come on," shouted the supervisor. "This way. We ain't paying you to sit on your can." He waved his hands frantically and his face reddened, exposing fat blue veins on his neck and forehead. Then he mumbled something and hurried away, screaming at the man in the crane to the amusement of the other workers.

Tomas smiled. He pulled out a cigarette and placed it between his lips. Then he picked up his welding gun and squeezed the trigger gently. A snakelike tongue of silver wire projected outward from the tubular mouth and trembled in the rusty air. He touched the metal bar with the wire and there was a burst of fire, yellow and blue.

Tomas sighed. He held the cigarette against the scarlet tip of wire and inhaled. Then he pulled the face guard over his face and the world was far removed. Darkness alone existed, as he imagined it was in the beginning of Time; as the old padres had told him it was in Hell, when he had been an orphan in a Mexican monastery. He loved the alone feeling. It gave him a chance to be his real self.

He touched the metal bar again and there was a spark of electricity and a ball of sunshine, warm and golden. The light flickered orange shadows against the gray factory walls and magnified his own shadow to monstrous proportions. Tomas laughed inwardly. It was like being God and creating the sun again, or being the first man to make fire. He loved the feeling. He loved wielding the miniature sun in his hands. He loved the alone feeling it gave him. But he also would love his new job.

He touched another rod and watched the rusted iron melt and run in thick silver puddles. He went to another rod and did the same. The joist began to take form.

He welded another rod and thought of his wife and how proud she was over his promotion; she had actually said so. He hummed a song and welded two more rods. He thought of buying a new car and moving to a better neighborhood. The thoughts were all pleasing, all possible now.

Another rod and another and another, back and forth, up and down, and the day burned away. He remembered the time he had wanted to be a bullfighter. Even now, the thought brought a warm surge of excitement to his blood, a hopeless yearning for those lost days. But he rapidly dismissed the melancholy feeling. The past was gone and should be buried. Margarita always said that. Besides, it had been hard being an orphan. He was married now and into better times. The hours drifted away.

Tomas raised his face mask and took a deep drag off his stubby cigarette. Then he let it drop to the floor in a rain of pink cinders and stepped on it casually.

"Hey, Manuel, you better hurry up," he called to his partner opposite him.

The other lifted up his face mask. "Yeah, what's the hurry?" he asked.

"They're not satisfied with our production upstairs. They say we're going to have to speed up down here, or else."

"Or else what?"

Tomas shrugged. "The unemployment office, I guess." He laughed.

"Well, you know what they can do with their factory. I ain't going to kill myself for no gringo."

Tomas nodded, thoughtfully. He had forgotten about Manuel.

Manuel came over and stood beside him. "Hey, take over for me. I'm going to the john." He winked. "Gotta take a little break."

"Mano, I don't think you should be taking so many breaks. The head supervisor doesn't like it."

"So? You're going to be in charge pretty soon, aren't you?"

Tomas hesitated. "Yes, but. . . ."

"All right men, break it up and get to work," said an authoritative voice. It was the head supervisor.

Tomas's face reddened. Manuel brought his body to attention and mock saluted. "Yes, sir," he said, laughing. He waited until the supervisor had walked away, then turned to Tomas and made a face.

Tomas shrugged. He pulled the steel mask over his face and shut out the outside world again. He needed to be alone with himself. He needed to think. He had forgotten about Manuel and the other men who had voted him foreman. He touched another rod with the wire. The lights sputtered and hurled out sparks like fireflies into the darkness. They fell at his feet and died slowly, burning into his already scarred shoes.

Tomas whistled. He purposely thought of drowsy sun-baked villages in Mexico. Maybe now he would be able to save enough for a vacation. Margarita would like that. Maybe he could even take her to Mexico, to a real bull ring. But she would not like the ring. He would take her to Mexico City instead. He sang a Spanish song and welded another rod.

The time passed slowly. Tomas pulled the helmet off and wiped his forehead on his shirt sleeve then glanced up at the clock.

He lit another cigarette and welded two more joists.

Finally, the bell rang. "Break time!" someone shouted. The machines silenced, slowly and whining, their huge steel mouths frozen in the act of chewing.

Tomas lifted the helmet from his head and laid it gently on the table. He pulled off his burnt gloves, wiped off his grimy face, and brushed back his hair. Then he picked up the lunch box and pulled out the warm thermos and a sandwich. He went and sat outside on a wooden bench by a giant pine tree. The canal drifted aimlessly below. It was milky green now. Louis, Alberto, and Manuel came over and sat next to him.

"Eh, Tomas, tomorrow's the big day, huh?"

Tomas nodded and smiled.

"Can you imagine that," said Alberto. "Our own quiet Tomas."

"Eh, muchachos," said Manuel. "Now when we get one of our own blood to be boss, things will be a lot better for us, no?"

Young Manuel laughed.

The others nodded and laughed, too.

Tomas remained silent. He took a bite out of the tortilla sandwich and munched thoughtfully on it.

"Congratulations, Tomas," said Alberto.

"We must celebrate!" chirped Louis.

"Sí," they all agreed.

"Hey Tomas, remember those times we used to come to work half drunk from those all night parties? Those were real celebrations, eh?"

Tomas nodded nostalgically. "Ah, yes, but that was a long time ago, amigos. Long before I got married."

"Ah, yes," they all agreed, rather wistfully.

There was silence for a few minutes.

"Well, what about the celebration?" someone asked.

"Yeah," said Manuel. "What do you say, Tomas? We get drunk tonight or no?"

Tomas's face reddened. "I'm sorry, but I can't go tonight. I promised Margarita we would go looking for a new apartment," he said.

"You're moving, eh?"

Tomas nodded.

"Where to?" asked Manuel.

Tomas hesitated. "The Lakeview area maybe."

"Hey, that's a classy section," someone said.

"Maybe some other night, then," said Louis.

"Yes, some other night," said Tomas.

There was a long pause in the conversation. Then Louis spoke again. "Hey, Tomas, what are you going to do about Manuel when you become foreman? He spends more time in that john than he does welding."

Everyone laughed, including Tomas.

Manuel threw his arm around Tomas and patted him on the back vigorously. "Are you kidding?" he said. "Tomas and me are almost brothers. Why, before he got married, we used to share the same women. Remember, Tomas?"

Tomas smiled and nodded. "Ah, yes," he sighed. "Those were good days, weren't they?"

"See?" laughed Manuel.

The other men smiled and nodded their heads, but said nothing. Then a fellow worker came over and tapped Tomas on the shoulder.

"Hey, the supervisor says to report to the office. Mr. Jerome is waiting to see you. He said you can finish your break when you come back, *Mr.* Sanchez." He winked at the others, and they all laughed. But Tomas only smiled.

"Well," he said.

His friends wished him luck. Tomas folded the sandwich neatly and placed it back in the lunch box. Then he spilled the coffee from his cup and screwed the cup back onto the thermos.

He stood up very slowly and glanced around at his friends' copper faces. They were all looking up at him. It was funny, Tomas thought. He hadn't realized before how old they were all getting. He looked beyond them to the nimbus clouds forming in the pale summer sky. A cool, rainy breeze swept across the canal and rustled the pine needles overhead.

Tomas turned and started walking away slowly, thinking out his every step. He heard his friends' laughter dying behind him, and he hesitated one last time.

Then he remembered Margarita and the promotion, and he hurried forward.

Christopher Dow

Rimbeau's Women

ART IS AN ILLUSION OF the senses, but one does not merely see the lifelike qualities of the painting or statue, nor do musical pieces please the ear alone. Words put together, whether denotatively or connotatively, are not merely descriptive. In truth, the illusions of art lie not in the deception of the senses, for the senses are fooled easily enough, as any parlor magician can demonstrate. It is the deception of those deeper receptive agents within the intellect and emotions that is more difficult to accomplish, whether the art work is naturalistic or not. Were this not the truth, all art that is not literal would be impossible as well as inexplicable.

But after all, we have the Surrealists, the Cubists, and the Abstract Expressionists, and the rise of these schools of art indicates that humans often have needs and goals that go beyond fundamental devotion to observable nature. We encounter particular emotional and intellectual responses to the stimulation of a given art work, whether the painting is photorealistic or fields of color, the music is a romantic interlude or atonal jazz, or the literature consists of expository writing or stream of consciousness. The sensations, ideas, and feelings engendered by a piece of art can be agreeable or not, but for a piece to be valid as art, they simply must relate significantly in all three spheres. This is the essence of art, not faithful reproduction. Faithful reproduction is just a style. The real question is how does the artist accomplish intellectual and emotional deception? I have an incident to relate that will suggest one possible answer.

It concerns Edward Rimbeau, the recently deceased artist, and took place twenty years ago. Since the subject concerns the nudes he became so famous for, you might say that the story does not apply to art that is not naturalistic, but I believe it can and does apply to all art. No doubt, Miro's shapes and colors meant no less to Miro than Rimbeau's nudes did to Rimbeau, though I'm sure in a different way.

Rimbeau had always been highly praised as a realist of the first order. His works brought not only a high price but critical acclaim. Then the women appeared, and afterward he painted nothing else. At any showing of Rimbeau's works, guests politely made the rounds of the landscapes, the seascapes, the cityscapes, and the other past escapes of Rimbeau's psyche, and everyone remarked how well Rimbeau painted, how lifelike, as if what you saw was not a plane of canvas but a window into the world. What everyone was really remarking, the men with lust and the women with envy, was just how well Rimbeau painted women, and each visitor managed to return to the women a second, a third, or even a fourth time to stare or gawk up at them. And why not? Women seem to bring out Rimbeau's genius more than landscapes or what have you. Rimbeau is not Gainsborough or Constable. Rimbeau paints women, so look, revel, enjoy his excellence!

I admit I'd done my own share of staring. I considered Rimbeau's women to be creatures of perfection, more real, passionate, and beautiful than any women I had ever seen. Life-sized and more true than the woman standing next to you, they seemed to stare out of the canvases, to look right into your eyes, to infuse your desires with some spark of their passions. Though they were nudes, there was nothing lewd or obscene about them, nothing to jolt the sensibilities or tease desire. Rather, there existed about them an aura of life and glorification of the body so subtle yet so strong that you forgot the people around you, forgot that the women were on canvas, in fact, nearly forgot that you were not and never could be as perfect or flourishing as they.

Rimbeau was in his early forties at the time of this particular show. He was of ordinary stature, and his features were a trifle sharp though in a rather pleasant and sensitive way. He was balding above the forehead, a fact that a rival painter joked was the result of long hours of hair tearing over incomplete canvases. Rimbeau countered that, in reality, he had plucked the hair from his head during late nights so he wouldn't have to wait until morning to obtain new brushes. Such a reply was typical of Rimbeau, who was neither the most brilliant nor the dullest of wits. Only his eyes were remarkable. They were a sort of blue-black, as if the pupils had enlarged and swallowed the irises, as if they were optical singularities somehow devouring the visual world.

Soon after I arrived at the gallery, I saw Rimbeau standing between a portrait of a city and a seascape's crashing wave. For some reason I had never fathomed, he did not like to be near his women during a show. He would supervise their hanging and then not see them until he came to take them down. It was almost as if he was embarrassed in their presence. They also had, I knew, the power to embarrass him out of their presence. Now, as I approached him, I could see they were about to do so again.

A young woman I recognized as being from an affluent family stepped up to him just as I arrived. She was very good looking, and I could guess what was going to happen. With small talk I did my best to help Rimbeau out of his predicament, and he tried very hard to skirt the subject of the women, but the young lady was persistent and finally had her way.

"You paint women beautifully, Mr. Rimbeau. So real and true to nature."

Rimbeau nodded his thanks, and the young lady went on.

"I wonder, could you use a model? I have some experience at sitting. I sat for Gregory Williams, you know. Maybe you've seen the picture? It's hanging in the Bellefontaine Collection."

"I've seen it," Rimbeau replied, and as he did, I remembered the painting. It was an excellent piece of craftsmanship, with the right amount of subtlety to raise it from being merely a well-executed picture of a pretty girl to an enchanting and provocative visual delight. It was not a Rimbeau, of course, but it was very nice.

"It is a wonderful painting," Rimbeau continued. "And you are very lovely, but I'm afraid I haven't a need for models right now."

"Yes, very lovely," the girl said wistfully. "But I'm not like your women, am I, Mr. Rimbeau?" She smiled at him. "I'm not...beautiful like they are."

"Beauty is in the eye of the beholder," Rimbeau quoted, fixing his gaze on the girl's face. "And, I think, it requires a certain maturity. In ten years, if you treat yourself the right way, you will have the beauty of the women I paint."

The girl blushed. Her eyes dropped then moved back to Rimbeau's face.

"Where do they come from? I mean, where do you find your models?" she asked.

"My friend here," Rimbeau put his hand on my arm, "has been, until this moment, the only person with whom I have shared this secret. Now I will share it with you, but you must promise never to tell anyone." What followed was the truth, and as far as I knew, I was the only person who knew it.

The girl nodded, so Rimbeau went on.

"There are no models. All my paintings come from my mind alone."

"But they're so lifelike. You must go by something...."

"Yes, but it is the convolutions of my psyche, not the contours of real flesh that guide me. The only reality my women have is as you see them. They are born on my palette, and they mature on the canvas. I watch them grow, and I give them life. Then I give them to the world."

"So beautiful, so perfect...."

"If they are, it is because they are my children, and I love them and want them to be beautiful and perfect. The only difference between you and them is that you are born real, with all the flaws and frailties of real flesh. My women are born an image, an ideal in my mind, and so are perfect before they become real."

Rimbeau stopped and turned his dark eyes to stare vacantly in the direction of his women. Then he faced the girl again.

"It may well be," he said, "that, in truth, you are the more perfect, for your perfection came after the idea of you. Your perfection is the labor of love; that of my women is simply the love of labor."

The girl averted her eyes for a moment before she said, "Perhaps I could watch you paint sometime."

A shadow of pain crossed his strange eyes. I don't think the girl saw it, but I did, then and once before when I had of him the same request. I anticipated his reply and the girl's sadness, and his reply when it came returned the sadness to me from where I had hidden it so long before. Who would not be saddened to be denied by a god the privilege of watching him create?

"I'm sorry," he said, "but it is too personal a matter."

"Yes...I...." She blushed, then, as she saw the pain, and she turned and gracefully fled.

Rimbeau faced me, and I looked into his strange eyes and could see in their darkness all of my own sorrow mirrored, magnified. I wished the subject had not risen again to plague me. I had believed all that hunger shelved far back in my mind.

"We are old friends," he implored me. "You would not hold this one thing against me?"

I wouldn't, I knew, but I felt that if I stayed right now, I might starve in the black holes of his eyes.

"No, but I, too, must go."

"Please try to understand...," he called softly after me as I fled from him, from the gallery; fled to some gaily lit and tinseled section of town. On this Saturday night, I hoped the sight of boisterous men and women might dispel all thought of Rimbeau's women. But the truth cannot be denied—what I desired of all things in the world, or above or below, was to touch one of Rimbeau's women. I want to take one of them—any one, which did not matter—into my arms, caress her, give her my love.

It did not matter that Rimbeau had said to me any number of times that he used no models or that I once had him watched to ascertain the truth of this statement. Not once during the course of several weeks did he take a woman to his rooms, nor did he see any, yet during that time, out of those same rooms came three of his women. I am not sure what I believed. Perhaps I thought he kept a woman in his apartment, though I'd been there often enough to know this was not the case. Yet I also knew that such reality, such life, could not come from nothing. I was convinced that he had to base his pictorial visions on something more than fantasy.

What I can see now but could not then was my own fantasy. I hoped that some of the power of Rimbeau's expression would be invested not only in the painting, but in the model herself. If I could possess, at least for a short time, one of his models, perhaps I could also possess, vicariously, Rimbeau's power. I was, however, blind to myself—or blinded under the spell of all the women Rimbeau had produced. He had created, amazingly, one of his life-sized women a week for the last three years. It was a phenomenal pace, but one he had, it seemed, worked into a fine science. He kept a strict schedule, beginning a canvas on Monday and finishing it on Saturday. On Sunday he relaxed and showed me his latest creation. I was always the first to see a fin-ished work, but now, as I sat at a bar, surrounded by shallow and tawdry shadows of Rimbeau's women, I resolved that, this time, I would see the model he painted from.

I paid for my fifth drink, left the bar, and made my way to Rimbeau's address. I saw by my watch that I had more than an hour before the showing was over—an hour in which to explore for myself, at last, the truth of Rimbeau's assertion that he had no models. I ascended the stairs to his apartment, found the spare key I knew he kept hidden, and let myself in.

The lights in the apartment were on, and I thought, ah! the model is here! But she was not in any of the rooms. Finally, I came to the studio, my heart pounding, knowing she was in there, waiting for Rimbeau, thinking me Rimbeau come, waiting.... But the only item of significance in the studio was the easel, lightly draped with cloth. My chagrin at not finding Rimbeau's model vanished before the anticipation of seeing his next painting. I gen-tly lifted the cloth covering.

I don't believe I have ever been so disappointed in my life as I was at the sight of that canvas. It was a lovely painting of a lovely, and yes, beautiful woman, executed in masterful brush strokes, with a tonal quality and texture that could only belong to smooth, soft skin covering real, firm flesh. It was as perfectly poised a painting as that which Williams had painted of the girl who approached Rimbeau earlier in the evening. It was definite-ly by Rimbeau—all the marks were there, as plain to the eye as the luster of her dark hair—but it wasn't really a Rimbeau. That special quality of truth, reality—call it what you will—just wasn't there, though the painting was photographically perfect.

Well, almost photographically perfect. Small sections here and there were not quite completed, including a portion of her foot and areas of her lustrous hair as well as the space where he signed his paintings. Could these small bits of imperfection explain the lack of life? No, I knew the explanation could not be contained in so simple a solution.

Rimbeau had lost his touch.

The moment the thought entered my mind, I tried to batter it down, tried to push from me the reality of that sudden, terrible conviction. I believe now my violent reaction was born out of the sense of loss I could not help but feel, for never again, I realized, would I ever see a Rimbeau woman in quite the same way. Never again could I even touch one with my eyes. Oh, there were all the ones he'd painted already, just as desirable and beautiful as always, but somehow their magic was dulled. It was as if Rimbeau himself were dead, and with his passing, all the true beauty of his paintings had passed also.

But that raised a sticky possibility. Could it be that art was art only because in it was invested some element of the artist's own vitality, something that went deeper than pictorial perfection or intellectual and emotional expression? Was there a sort of psychic bond between the artist and his work? But if that were the case, wouldn't the truth of any piece of art die with the artist? And I knew that wasn't so. Great works live on long after the artist's demise because of their intrinsic worth. No, that wasn't right, either. If it were, then the masterworks of the past would have as much meaning for a modern viewer as for a contemporary of the artist, and I knew that was not necessarily the case. My first thought must be correct: Art is invested with the artist's vitality, and if the work lives beyond the artist's lifetime, then it is due to the intensity of that vitality somehow preserved within the artwork. No, no, that was crazy, too, else the scrawlings of a madman would be as valid as sketches by Rembrandt.

I was confused. It was as if Rimbeau's loss of ability was my own loss of comprehension. One can define motifs, devices, cultural significance, or any number of terms to explain the impact of a work of art on an individual, but in the end, the impact itself cannot be defined. Then, as I was trying to define the impact that Rimbeau's lost touch had on me, the street door opened, and I heard Rimbeau's step on the stairs.

I must have been drunker than I thought for the time to have passed so quickly, but I was not too drunk to realize he must not find me here. He who had never let another look upon his work before it was complete must not suffer the anguish of being found lacking by some artistic voyeur. I re-covered the painting and hid in the studio closet, thinking to sneak out as soon as he went to bed. Also, I'm sure, the desire to watch him work a little, even if he had lost his touch, was strong in me. Or, uglier, perhaps it was jealousy of something he once had but I would never have that made me stay to view in secret triumph his loss of that quality. So I hid in the closet, leaving the door open the slightest amount and positioning myself so I could comfortably see the easel.

His familiar figure entered the room and went straight to the easel and lifted the cloth. There he stood for several minutes, staring at the woman before him. I could not see his full face from where I was and so could not read his expression. But evidently his will had not abandoned him as had his touch, for, picking up a brush, he began painting.

He worked tinily, deftly, and with a great intensity, his hand jumping from palette to canvas, from one incomplete area of the painting to another and back to the palette. Now and then, he would pause and step back or squint sideways at the canvas, and each time, his return was more vigorous and, somehow, more aberrant, for the delicacy of his strokes belied the dynamic vigor with which his body moved. He seemed literally to dance in a sort of hypnotic rhythm before the easel. His exertions caused him to break into a sweat, and the moisture highlighted his cheekbones and glistened along his brow. Presently, he put his brush down and removed his shirt. As he did, I was startled by three things.

The first was the amount Rimbeau was sweating. I, in my closet, must have been much hotter than he, but where I was merely damp, Rimbeau's torso was drenched with a thick swelter. The second was the incredible change that the past hour had wrought on the canvas. I had been a fool to think Rimbeau had lost his touch. What I had seen before was merely the sketch, the foundation, the embryo from which life emerged. He had told the girl that his women matured on the canvas, and I had become witness to the truth of that statement. The canvas was now at least half as alive as any of the finished works I had seen. She seemed to poise there in front of Rimbeau as if she wanted to climb down off the easel. Third, I realized that Rimbeau must be mad; that I, in hiding and watching him work, had witnessed the insanity he had managed to conceal from the world, even from me.

As he turned and threw his shirt from him, I caught a glimpse of his full face, his eyes, and I was sure of my diagnosis. His features looked oddly discolored, at once flush and pale, and his eyes, those dark pools, were now glowing dimly, as if all the light they had devoured was luminating forth. I'd heard that the bodies of maniacs were capable of superhuman feats, and I shuddered least he discover me watching him. But I made no noise, and he turned back to his easel.

The ugly sweat now poured off him, and life streamed from his brush as he attacked the canvas in a near fury of devotion and concentration. Soon, he was radiating so much heat that I, in my closet, began to sweat heavily, too, and it stung my eyes and blurred my sight, but I was afraid to move, afraid to wipe it away, terrified of being discovered.

I blinked, and from his brush the strokes brought life, amazingly. The sweat was running from my hair and into my eyes now, and through the salty haze, I thought I saw his sweat mingle with the pigment, the pigment with his sweat, until he seemed to be painting with himself. He paused, plucked a single hair from his head, and, with his brush, stroked it into her tresses. Then he arched upward, kissed the beautiful lips, returned to his brush, and was it the light or the sweat of the heat and energy, or...her lips were so real! And as he delicately finished a toenail, caressing her arm all the while, why did the hair on my arm prickle? Where did his canvas end? When did I sleep and the illusion of thick, glossy hair cascading over Rimbeau's shoulder occur? Did he and she seem to fall together because it was I who fell?

Rimbeau's apartment was silent when I stumbled from the closet the next morning. He had gone to meet me for our accustomed Sunday morning breakfast. But the apartment was not empty. I could feel the presence of the painting, and I tried to look at it, but a sense of guilt and grief permitted me only an ashamed glance. That one brief look showed me the same yet now awful beauty that I had always seen but never understood, but it now divulged a terrible truth. With that realization came the certainty of my own contrite departure from the world where Rimbeau's women reign supreme.

I did not meet Rimbeau for breakfast. In fact, I never saw him again, though he tried often enough to get in touch with me during the years until his premature death. Nor have I again seen one of his women. I am certain the intensity with which I felt that final painting was not due to that particular painting but was simply invested in them all, where a discerning eye could easily see. Rimbeau's women, it is true, are visions of loveliness, but I think of Rimbeau's words to the pretty young girl, and I wonder if the rewards were worth their price.

Steven Robinson

The Field Trip

LOUIS HILL PEERED ANXIOUSLY DOWNWARD, hoping to catch his first real glimpse of the Ozark Mountains, now held in a shroud of thick morning fog. He had crossed the range only three days before, traveling north but in the pitch of night could only feel their presence, these Ozarks, the first mountains he would ever see. As it was, only occasional patches of transparent haze allowed him any view at all. He could see trees, stand upon stand, forming giant slopes, but without the richness and diversity of shade that nature provided them. Nor could he see mountain tops arch into clear sky in elegant contrast or the valley floors and their passes. He could only imagine the panoramas. Louis Hill was away from home for the first time on a working field trip for his employers, Masters Protective Services.

The car snaked down the narrow mountain road, little more than a series of hairpin turns, and Louis's supervisor, John Seaton, took them skillfully, driving well beyond the speed limit so prudently recommended by the State of Arkansas. Seaton was in a hurry and would not be delayed by low visibility or bad roads. Louis heard a gasp from the back seat and turned to see that Oly Allen had gone white. Oly, the third member of the party, was a thin, middle aged woman, given to nervous tension, and she was shaken now.

"Please slow down, John," she asked.

"Relax, Oly," Seaton replied. "I'm an excellent driver, and if you want to get home tomorrow night, we have to stay on schedule."

Louis closed his eyes from the haze and felt confident that no accident would befall them today, for they owned the road, such as it was. Not another soul was driving, for it was

169

Christmas day. There was one more stop in Shreveport, Louisiana, and then they would head for home.

As they made their way out, Louis wondered how he came to be in this place, with these people who were little more than strangers to him. Of course, it was simple. He needed a job badly. He took home eighty dollars a week to provide an opportunity for people to steal. He had spent the last eight weeks running the exact change ruse on unsuspecting clerks in drug and department stores, restaurants and grocery chains, attempting to reach the expected quota of four "catches" a day. The survival of the new Masters office in Houston depended on producing a respectable number of crooks, and whether they were hard-up cosmetics counter girls or desperate hardware salesmen, it really made little difference. Louis hated these shopping tours and feared most of all the object of his mission —the catch. He rode each day with crews of women, hard unattractive women of prison guard mentality, who berated him constantly for his lack of aggressiveness. He tired of buying ties, aftershave, and cans of Raid, only to throw the merchandise into the trunk of the car to be returned to the office at the end of the day. He was equally weary of buying three lunches a day and doling out egg rolls and pizzas to the incredulous and distrustful service station attendants. How could one explain that the food was okay? There were reports to fill out and receipts to reconcile in this morass of a third-rate secret agency, but the trip came up, and Louis decided he would stay on a little longer. Five days of shopping accounts in Louisiana and Arkansas had taken them from Lake Charles to Fayetteville and south to Little Rock and El Dorado, and they had remarkably averaged one catch a day. Louis witnessed his first interrogation three days into the trip in Harrisonville, Arkansas. The subject of the interview was a woman in her eighties, a clerk in one of ITT's Continental Bakeries. Situated in a rural area, the shop specialized in selling day-old products, bread, and sweet rolls. The woman apparently took just over three dollars of the multinational's sales during the test. An astute and cautious inquisitor, John Seaton was confident he could get a confession from her, but even his reversion into the Stalin School of Tactics failed him. The woman only admitted making an error and the session ended inconclusively with the Continental management opting to take over the matter. Louis secretly admired the woman's indignant resistance, and when no one else was watching, he wished her good luck.

"Leave me alone," she said, her wrinkled white face impassive, her tone frigid.

As they sped south toward Louisiana, Louis wondered how the old woman was spending her Christmas.

*

"Hi, folks, my name is Tony Roy, and I hope you're enjoying your stay at Pines View Lodge. I'm here to play your favorite tunes, and I want to kick off this last set with one of my favorites."

Tony Roy sang.

"By the time I get to Phoenix, she'll be rising. . . ."

Louis sipped his second Bacardi and coke and took in the decor of the Wilderness Club, resplendent in ersatz wood grain and red vinyl. He was loose and felt pleased to be of age in Louisiana, for he was impatient in adolescence, sensing from a tender age that success would only come to him as an adult. At the moment he felt like one, albeit a slightly drunken one.

"Are you enjoying yourselves?" Seaton asked as he sipped scotch and water.

"Oh, it's very nice," said Oly. "Especially the music. He's a good singer, don't you think?"

Seaton nodded in polite assent as his eyes surveyed the room. Mindlessly he began tapping his glass on the table, and then he spoke.

"Let's drink to our success—five catches in five days. You've done well."

Louis was embarrassed at this show of mock camaraderie. Little had passed between them in the past week, and everyone knew it. Seaton spoke again.

"We just have one more assignment which we will take care of in the morning, and then we'll be on our way back to Houston."

"What kind of place are we shopping?" Louis asked.

"It's a Singer Sewing shop right downtown. There will probably be two clerks, so the best thing to do will be to run a correct change test with you going first, Oly, and Louis following you."

Seaton continued to talk, but Louis found himself unable to pay attention to the words. He was tired of Seaton, of the way he talked, and longed to be someplace else. He studied his supervisor. Seaton was perhaps six feet tall and of slender build, with sandy hair graying at the temples. He nevertheless retained the look of a petulant child. During his enforced confinement with this man, Louis concluded that Seaton's function was little more than that of a confidence man, running a game on clients, subordinates, and everyone else. What really bothered Louis was that like other con men, this incorrigible promoter of security schemes and oily character at large moved easily in the world, a world Louis was stumbling to assimilate without success. Louis wanted to succeed, but he knew he could never be like the John Seatons of the world.

"Louis, didn't you say you used to sing in a band?" asked Oly.

"Yeah, that's right," said Louis.

"Why don't you get up there and sing a song?" said Seaton.

"Oh, I don't know, it's been a while, besides, I don't know what to sing."

Seaton excused himself and, to Louis's horror, went over and spoke to Tony Roy. As quickly as he left, he returned and before Louis could speak, he heard Tony Roy say, "We have a young man in the audience who sings with a band in Houston, Texas, and he's going to come up and do a song for you right now."

The people in the room, half full, applauded dutifully.

Louis felt his stomach knot up and his mouth go dry.

"Go on, Louis," said Oly. "It'll be fun."

Louis looked at John Seaton, who said, "C'mon Louis, break a leg."

An external force seemed to move him out of his chair, and he made his way with mechanical steps to the stage.

"What's your name?" asked Tony Roy.

"Louis Hill."

"What number would you like to do?"

Louis screamed inside, what song did he know the words to?

"Uh, how about 'Let It Be Me'?" he mumbled.

"Okay, by the Everly Brothers. Now what key do you sing in?"

"Well, I'm not exactly sure, just let me hear one and maybe I can tell."

Roy played a chord on the piano, and Louis said, "That'll be okay."

"Folks, this is Louis Hill and he's going to do a hit ballad made famous by the Everly Brothers—'Let It Be Me'."

Louis heard himself sing:

> "Don't ever leave me lonely
> Tell me you love me only
> And that you'll always, let it be me."

Something was wrong, but he couldn't tell exactly what it was.

> "Each time we meet, love, I find complete love,
> Without your sweet love, what would life be?"

The applause was polite and restrained, and now Louis knew he had made a mistake.

"Well, I guess Mr. Hill can be forgiven for being a little off key tonight. Let's give him an E for effort."

Louis shook hands with Roy and returned to his seat. To his surprise, he didn't care if he made a fool of himself. He was going home tomorrow.

*

Around eight thirty the next morning, a bright yellow sun shone on downtown Shreveport's Main Street. Louis, along with Oly Allen and John Seaton, was waiting for breakfast in Poole's Pharmacy. Louis was sipping coffee, nursing a slight hangover, and as usual, growing tense just before shopping an account. The fear of catching some poor fool pocketing small change and the subsequent ritual of interrogation chilled him to the bone, but he could say nothing, certainly not in the company of his colleagues.

They ate breakfast in silence, paid the check, and walked out to the car.

John Seaton said, "I'll park down the street from the Singer store, and Oly will go in first. Now Oly, before you make your buy, wait until you see Louis. We'll give you a couple of minutes to pick something out."

"It doesn't matter what I buy?" asked Oly.

"No, anything you can pay for in correct change, but try to keep it under ten dollars. When you see Louis, give him a chance to pick up the layout of the store, and Louis, you make sure you're with her when she gives her money to the clerk."

"Okay," said Louis.

Then he saw it, just on the corner—the Singer Sewing Center.

"Okay," said Seaton. "Go ahead."

Louis got out of the front seat of the car, and Oly emerged at the same time from the back.

"Not yet, Louis," scolded Seaton.

Louis stopped in his tracks. Fortunately, the car was not parked directly in front of the store. Louis returned to the car and got in beside Seaton.

"That's a good way to blow a test, Louis," said Seaton.

"Look, John!" Louis said sharply. "There are so many people on the street, I could hardly have been noticed, and besides, I didn't walk in front of the store."

"Okay, okay, relax. We'll give Oly one more minute."

Louis's anger receded as quickly as it had flared. He felt foolish.

"I guess I'm just anxious to get it over with," he told Seaton.

Seaton nodded in silence. Then he said, "Okay, Louis, go now."

Louis was out of the car again. The store was just up ahead on the left, and as he got closer to it, his heart began to pound, loudly enough, he thought, for anyone to hear. It was the same way every time. Louis was certain everyone knew his identity and purpose, seeing clearly through the subterfuge and sham acting. He found it almost impossible to look people in the eyes. Finally, he stood in front of the store and through its window saw Oly examining patterns. He also saw a man and a woman behind the checkout counter. He pulled the door open and entered. The woman was engrossed in discussion with a customer, while the man, in his fifties and of stocky build, seemed to be studying receipts. Louis was relieved for had someone approached him offering assistance, he would have had not idea what to ask for.

He walked to the hardware section. He had to decide quickly what to buy. Scissors, he would buy scissors, an item a man could ask for without betraying ignorance of sewing. Louis knew nothing of needles or bobbins but could easily justify a need for scissors to the clerk. He looked at Oly to let her know that she could make her buy. He cursed under his breath when he saw what Oly held in her hands. A pair of scissors just like the ones he had picked up.

Suddenly the female clerk was upon him.

"Sir, may I help you?" she asked.

Louis quickly replaced the scissors.

"Thread," he said. "Uh, red thread, a couple of spools."

"The thread is just over here. Follow me," the woman said. "What type did you want?"

"Oh, cotton will be all right."

Louis hoped that Oly could stall until he could free himself and cover the cash register. The male clerk remained behind the counter.

"Will this do?" the woman asked.

"Yeah, that's fine."

The woman looked at him with a quizzical expression. He forced a smile and said. "A trick."

"What?"

"A magic trick, that's what I use the thread for."

"Oh, well, Mr. Henderson will take care of you."

"Thanks very much."

As he moved toward the register, he heard Oly speak to Mr. Henderson.

"What is the tax on these?" She held out the scissors.

"Thirty-three cents, ma'am."

"Here you are. My husband is waiting in the car."

She put eight dollars and thirty-two cents on the counter, and turning on her heels, quickly left the store.

Louis held himself far enough away from the counter to be unobtrusive and observed Mr. Henderson. The clerk did not open the register, for the reading of the last sale remained, four dollars and eighteen cents. If Henderson didn't put the money in the register, where was it? As Louis walked up to the counter, he was afraid he knew.

"That'll be seventy-nine cents, sir," smiled Mr. Henderson.

"Here you are," said Louis, and gave Henderson a dollar bill.

They had another catch, for Louis was certain that Henderson had the money in his pocket. This was the most flagrant thievery yet to occur on the trip. He walked coolly out of the store and as he approached the car, his excitement mounted. Without hesitation, he told Seaton and Oly, "We have a catch!"

Oly squealed, "He didn't ring up my money?"

"No, I'm certain of that," Louis replied.

"Did you see what he did with it?" Seaton asked. His face flushed; he, too, was excited.

"It wasn't on the counter, and I know he didn't ring it up."

Seaton's eyes lit up and his face became a leer. "He put it in his pocket!"

"Yes, I think so," Louis said in a breathless tone.

"That's great, that makes six catches in six days! Now listen, I have to call the store manager and ask if he wants to handle the interrogation. You two wait in the car."

He wasted no time making his way to a phone.

"I just can't believe it," said Oly. "I wonder what will happen to him."

"If it goes like the others, he'll probably just be reprimanded."

The predatory euphoria Louis brought back to the car began to recede. He forgot himself for a few moments and performed his function coldly, but a vague apprehension now began to grip him, and he was afraid for the future of Mr. Henderson.

John Seaton appeared outside the car.

"We'll be meeting Mr. Marriot in twenty-five minutes. They want us to handle the interrogation."

"Who is he?" asked Oly.

"The store manager. Now Oly, why don't you have some lunch or do some window shopping? We'll meet you here in about an hour."

"I don't understand, John. Why can't I go with you?" she pleaded.

"Three people is too many, Oly, and besides, he could become hostile and even withdraw completely. It works best with two people."

Oly became sullen and remained silent.

"John, I would prefer not to go with you," said Louis.

Seaton became angry.

"You can't cope with this job if you can't deal with the questioning. This is your goddamn catch, and you're going with me!" His tone softened. "Louis, it's the only way you will ever get used to it."

Louis realized Seaton was right. It was his catch. He had to go.

"All right, John," he said, his tone resigned.

Stanley Marriot, a man of medium build in his early thirties, greeted them inside the store. His youngish face held a grim expression.

"I have him in my office. He doesn't know what's going on," said Marriot. "How are we going to do this?"

"First, we will ask him where the money is," Seaton said. "Have you balanced the register?"

"Yes, it checks."

"Then we know he didn't ring it up. When we confront him in this way, he will have no choice but to produce the stolen money. After we do that, we'll find out how much more he has stolen and over what span of time he has been taking it. Usually, a person will confess to stealing about half the money actually taken."

"You mean he may have been doing this regularly, I mean over a long period of time?" Marriot asked.

"You can be pretty sure of it," Seaton said. "But he will fill in the blanks for us." He turned to Louis. "Are you ready?" he asked.

"Yeah, I guess so," said Louis.

"Mr. Marriot, if you'll introduce us," Seaton said.

Marriot was hesitant. "You won't be too hard on him, will you?"

Seaton reassured him. "We only want to get the truth."

They walked into the office and found Mr. Henderson sitting in a chair opposite Marriot's desk. He was startled and at first didn't recognize Louis. He turned to speak to Marriot, but Marriot spoke first.

"George, these men are from the home office, and they have some questions to ask you."

Stanley Marriot was distinctly uncomfortable, his face ashen. If Henderson had any inkling of what was to come, he didn't reveal it.

"Mr. Henderson, my name is John Clark," Seaton lied, "and this is Louis Tyler. You may recall seeing Mr. Tyler earlier today."

Henderson looked at Louis and said to Seaton, "Yes, he made a purchase this morning—thread, I believe." Henderson was calm and very polite.

"That's right," said Seaton.

Louis remained silent.

Seaton then asked, "Do you recall the customer you attended just prior to helping Mr. Tyler?"

Louis saw a trace of panic cross the expression of George Henderson's face, and, just as quickly, it was gone.

"I'm not sure. It think it was a woman."

"Do you remember what she bought?"

"I think she bought some scissors. Say, what's this all about?" Tension began to surface in Henderson's voice.

Stanley Marriot said, "Relax, George."

Then Seaton's voice cracked like a whip. "I think you know very well what this is about. Shall I tell you what we know?"

Henderson's composure was breaking down rapidly.

"I don't understand," he said.

"Then I'll explain," said Seaton. "The woman who bought those scissors from you this morning works with us. Do you remember how much those scissors cost?"

"Around eight dollars," said Henderson. His voice was brittle.

"Eight dollars and thirty-two cents to be exact," said Seaton. "Now, Mr. Tyler here," he continued pointing at Louis, "has told us that that money was never rung up on the cash register."

Henderson was now openly shaken. "Well, sometimes when you get real busy that happens. I guess I forgot." He nervously fingered his glasses.

Stanley Marriot said sadly, "George, the money is not in the register."

Seaton spoke softly, "George, did you put that money in your pocket? Do you have it now?"

Henderson's shoulders heaved. The tension melted from him. He said to Marriot, "I guess I just wasn't thinking."

He stood up and took from his pocket the $8.32, placing it on Marriot's desk. Then he looked at Louis.

Louis could not avert his eyes from those of George Henderson. He was surprised, for he could see no anger or hatred. Henderson seemed to look at him as though extending some unspoken sympathy or perhaps forgiveness. His eyes damp, Henderson removed his glasses and wiped his eyes with a handkerchief.

"Will I lose my job, Stanley?" he asked.

"It's not my decision," said Marriot.

Seaton was only halfway into his questioning; he began to exploit his breakthrough with a more conciliatory approach.

"George," he said, "the best thing to do for yourself is to tell the truth. Now, how long has this been going on? Six months, a year, or longer?"

Louis began edging toward the door. He wanted to get out, outside where he could breathe.

"Just a couple of months. You know things haven't been going too well at home. I've had trouble making ends meet."

"Do you have any idea how much money you've taken over that period of time?"

Henderson did not answer.

"George, it's important that you tell us. You must have some idea," said Seaton.

Henderson sighed and said, "I'm not sure, Maybe a couple or three hundred dollars. But," he turned to the manager, "I could pay it back, Stanley. It wouldn't take long to do that."

Marriot said, "George, it depends on what the district manager says. We'll see."

Seaton spoke. "We're finished for now, Mr. Henderson. I wonder it you would mind stepping outside for a few moments?"

"Yes," said Stanley Marriot. "I'll talk to you in a few minutes, George."

Henderson rose heavily from his chair and made his way to the door. he seemed in a mild form of shock, the kind that overtakes the humiliated, the condemned. His eyes met Louis's a final time, and Louis now saw fear. Then Henderson was gone.

For the first time now, Seaton and Marriot sat down.

"This is terrible," said Marriot. "I just can't believe it's happening."

"It's always difficult to accept," said Seaton. "The best of employees can compromise themselves. It happens all the time, believe me."

"When I first took this job," said Marriot, "George helped me get over the rough spots. I'm not sure I could have made it without him. In that time, we've become friends. I just hope his tenure helps him."

"How long has he been here?" asked Louis.

"He received his fifteen year pin just two weeks ago," said Marriot.

There was silence in the room as Marriot picked up his phone to call the district manager in New Orleans. The call went through quickly, and the discussion was short.

"I've been told to fire him," said Marriot flatly.

"Just like that?" asked Louis.

"That's Sims for you, no mercy. Is there anything else?" Mariott asked. His tone became impersonal, his manner aloof.

"No," said Seaton. "We'll be sending our report on to New Orleans. We regret putting you in this unpleasant position, but we had no choice."

"I understand," said Marriot.

As Louis and Seaton left the store, Henderson was nowhere to be seen. Louis was relieved not to have to look in the man's eyes a final time. He thought of Henderson's family and was ashamed.

"Louis, you shouldn't feel responsible," said Seaton. "You did your job. The man was a thief."

"Yeah, you're right," said Louis.

Louis wondered what George Henderson would think if he knew they would both be looking for new jobs next week. Louis thought it would be little consolation.

The Relief of the Cat

LUNCH WAS GOOD AS USUAL. There was fried chicken, fresh from the yard, potatoes, greens, and cornbread. This was a country meal at its most profound, and the boy had grown used to such nourishment during a year's stay at his aunt's house. For John to clean his plate was not a dutiful gesture but a natural desire. His aunt was a fine cook, preparing food in much the same way as her mother and grandmother before her. She proceeded to wash the dishes directly after rising from the table, as was her custom.

"John, if you finish your homework this afternoon, I'll take you to the show tonight," she said as she dried a plate.

The boy's face fell at the mention of homework. He feared especially the arithmetic, remembering this weekend's assignment was unusually lengthy. Normally, it wouldn't have mattered so much, but at the Pine's theater this evening was the premier of *The Alamo,* starring John Wayne, and all his friends would be there. He had looked forward to this night for weeks, eagerly counting down the days.

"Don't worry, Auntie, I'll get finished. I don't have much," he lied.

His aunt was now preparing herself for work. She was a volunteer at Memorial Hospital. John sat on the bed and watched her as she brushed her hair, briskly, so as not to uncurl her permanent.

"If it's quiet tonight, I'll be home by six," she said as she walked through the front room and out of the door.

John followed her out to the car. "Have a nice afternoon, Auntie, and don't be late 'cause I'll be ready to go."

"Oh, John, don't forget to feed the dogs and Spooky," she said as she backed out of the dirt drive.

John watched her disappear down the road and decided to settle himself on the front porch to grapple with his homework.

Cold as it was, he preferred the outdoors to the confines of his room. First, history, he thought to himself.

He picked up a book. The history of the United States, the cover said, and he absently flipped the pages until he got to chapter twelve, entitled, "The Storm of Secession." The love seat rocked back and forth as he read.

Headline—*Boston Globe*—"Rebel guns fire on Fort Sumter in Charleston Harbor." John knew this material pretty well already, having read the chapters on the Civil War early in the semester. He was simply putting off the dreaded arithmetic as long as possible. The exploits of soldiers, frontiersmen, and cowboys took up most of his interest, and his thoughts again turned to the siege of the Alamo.

He saw Chuck amble from the side of the house to the front yard and curl himself up at the foot of a tall pine tree. Chuck was an old yellow dog, perhaps ten, and bore a remarkable resemblance to Disney's *Old Yeller*. He was broader in frame, but he shared the amiable disposition of the cinema dog. His head was broad and marked with scars and knots sustained in ancient battles with forgotten foes along Route 5, his domain. Chuck seldom had to fight now, except when a new dog came into the neighborhood. John had only witnessed two such incidents and neither could be considered fights in the strictest sense of the word.

Chuck was John's constant companion and had long since learned to get along with humans, growing up in a single family with the stable environment that experience provided him. He had a sweetness about him, being sublimely patient with children, stoically obliging those intent upon riding his back or tugging at his ears. He was neutral with cats, and though he probably chased them in his youth, only the gravest provocation would prompt him to do so now. His attitude toward dogs was decidedly more distinct. Chuck, like an old gunfighter, was a rare commodity. Dogs his age were generally arthritic and on the edge of senility, ill-fitted to answer the challenge of an aggressive pup hungry to stake ground. Though some speed was gone and the joints were stiff, the old yellow dog still kept his reputation and territory intact.

Chuck was dozing, curled up, head on forelegs. Then, turning on his back, he stretched all four limbs straight upward, tensed and then relaxed. John, laughing softly, put down his book as Chuck yawned, curling his tongue into a long arc, and sounding a breathless dog sigh. John jumped off the porch and approached Chuck saying, "I'm lazy as you are." The dog's thick tail began to wag as he got up to greet the boy. "Man," said John, as Chuck's tail hit his leg, "you could knock me down doin' that."

John looked across the pasture and saw the other dog his aunt kept on the place, Red, a three-year-old hound. Country people give their pets simple names. Red was born to the hunt, and what he lacked in steadiness of maturity, he made up for with speed and enthusiasm. He was playful and inquisitive, always looking for adventure and occasionally finding it. The sport he was currently enjoying was tormenting the neighbor's hounds. The neighbor in question, Mr. Leo Brown, kept in excess of a dozen hounds, caged behind his house. Red was bounding back and forth in front of the pen, yelling, barking, and stirring the caged pack into a frenzy.

The boy ran to the pasture fence whistling and shouting, "Red, Red, get over here." The young dog turned and casually loped toward the boy, oblivious to the scene of havoc left in his wake. "Damn you, dog," the boy scolded. "Old man Brown is gonna come after you with his shotgun one of these times."

Red wasn't the fighting type, lacking in both experience and inclination. He was more adept at running and, finding this an adequate defense, came to rely on it.

Since Red was just a puppy when he came to share a home with Chuck, there was never any rivalry between them. They sometimes roughhoused at Red's insistence, Chuck acceding in much the same way he would with any other child, but Red knew when Chuck didn't want to play. Red had, by now, stretched out beside his partner, and John, relishing the picture they made, had long ago decided their relationship was more than one of mutual tolerance.

The boy grudgingly worked on fractions for an hour and a half and suddenly remembered he hadn't fed the dogs. When mealtime was overdue, Chuck would fetch his empty dish to the nearest human and drop it at the person's feet. He made this gentle reminder to John with humble expression.

"Oh, I'm sorry boy," said John. "Let's go in the backyard, and I'll get you guys your supper." Red was already in the backyard in the early stages of his customary mealtime whimper. Their diet varied from processed dog food to scraps, but today it was scraps, which they seemed to prefer anyway. They gobbled their food without pretense, as dogs do, and at that point, Spooky the cat emerged from the garden wilds.

Spooky was as black as Red was red, and if the dogs possessed complimentary dispositions, the cat was naturally standoffish. His color suited a mystical nature—inscrutable as he was invisible at night, save two luminous eyes, cat eyes. They shone yellow-amber and seemed to John to hold innumerable secrets. Spooky displayed all the normal feline qualities, but defied predictability. One moment he could be coldly distant, and the next, playful and attention seeking. He was, however, never one to rub shins and, even hungry, would wait patiently for his supper without lowering himself to such indignity. He loved above all places the garden, sometimes remaining within its confines all day, totally absorbed, roaming through the corn and tomatoes stalking insects. He was ignored by Chuck, but Red would occasionally harass him, more as a diversion than calculated meanness. Red often chased cats, but really didn't know what to do in the event of cornering one, and the young cat, knowing how to defend himself, rarely went out of his way to avoid Red, or anything else, for that matter. These two even played, from time to time, but cautiously.

As the dogs ate, Spooky sat on his hindquarters a few feet away, intently watching their activity. He arched his back then walked slowly toward them, knowing just how close he could get. He, too, was ready to eat.

"C'mon, Spooky," John said, beckoning the cat into the house. Spooky ran across the backyard and bounded gracefully up the stone steps. John put a saucer of food down on the kitchen floor, and the cat began to eat. He took small bites, chewing thoroughly. His tail undulated hypnotically, signifying his contentment.

Everyone fed, John returned to the front porch, pleased that most of his homework was behind him. As he walked through the living room, the clock on the mantle chimed four. The dogs, appetites sated, resumed their siestas; Chuck again under his favorite tree and Red in a sunny spot adjacent to the woodpile, just opposite the stretch of pasture fence nearest the road.

"Finally," John spoke to himself as he closed his notebook. He stood up and rubbed his eyes. The rutted surface of Route 5 stretched before him, and there, in the distance, materialized the figures of four strange dogs, trotting in rude formation toward the house.

Chuck, usually slow moving, sprang to attention, ears up and nostrils flaring with the invaders' scent. Red would probably have run had not the pack descended on him so quickly. But they were suddenly on him, two of them, lunging at him from two directions.

The boy stood paralyzed as terror welled up inside him. Chuck charged the other two dogs and doing so, transformed himself into the wild creature which answers only the dictates of instinct. John saw years melt off the old dog, and a new taut figure assert itself, upright, enraged, and utterly vicious. The front yard, so long the frame of picnics and Easter egg hunts, was now a battlefield, a maelstrom of whirring shapes and primal fury.

They were just off the porch now, and John knew one or both of his dogs would die this day unless he intervened. But how? Then it came to him. He would have to get off the porch to the side of the house. He would turn the hose on them and from pure shock the attackers would break and run. The garden hose lay just a few feet down the side of the house, tied to the faucet.

Red was down now and overwhelmed. Once off its legs, it becomes impossible for any animal to carry on a fight, and no quarter would be shown today. Chuck was magnificent but wearing down fast. Move now, John thought to himself.

Suddenly, a black missile hurled across the space in front of him, as high as his head, landing squarely on the shoulders of one of Red's attackers, a big brown dog. Spooky, lurking in the hedge off the porch, had chosen his moment. John, stunned, watched in amazement as the dog bolted in blind panic toward the road, cutting the air with high-pitched shrieks. Spooky held fast to his mount, black cat ears pressed firmly against his head. Furious, he battered the dog's skull and ears. When he finally jumped off, the dog continued to run.

As an apparent result of the cat's audacious display, the remaining dogs seemed to lose the initiative, for Red found his feet and Chuck managed to beat off his attackers and run them out of the yard as well. Both of them sustained scratches and welts, but there were no serious wounds. Red immediately settled himself and tended his bruises, but Chuck posted himself near the road and surveyed its visible length, as though reliving the fight, a hundred fights. He soon looked his old self, and when John called to him, he walked over with his familiar expression, so akin to a human smile. Perhaps it was the old dog's pride.

Spooky sat near a rosebush, cleaning himself as casually as if he had merely been out in the garden with his insects. For him, the incident was forgotten, unimportant, all in a day's play. He began pawing the nearest branch, transfixed by the movement of the leaves in the late afternoon sunlight.

John spent a few minutes with his pets, looking them over, and satisfied they were all right, went into the house to get ready to see *The Alamo*. Somehow, he wasn't as excited as before about the movie. He had already witnessed the valor of sentinels.

Essays

Christopher Dow

The Ultimate Chicken

ONE EARLY MORNING, I FOUND myself sitting on a short flight of stone steps at the rear of an old stone and brick building. The building was atop the east side of a ridge, and before me spread a moderate-sized valley two or three miles wide and quite deep.

When I first sat, the valley was filled to the brim with a dense fog that seemed like an endless sea of white whose edges drifted up onto the lawn only a hundred or so feet away from me. Nothing tangible could be seen save the two towers of a church jutting above the surface a hundred yards down the hillside and the trees on the uppermost edge of the shrouded ridge across the valley. The sea was white and calm, the air above it quiet and still. The world was ethereal, and I was a sitter on its rocky verge.

From above the building at my back, the sun rose, illuminating first the opposite hilltop, then gradually the surface of the sea of mist filling the valley. As the sun's rays bathed the mist, shapes began to take form out of the blankness on the far slope, first in rough outline then in sharper detail. A tan patch soon acquired edges and turned into a house. A dark, foreshortened rectangle spotted with color became a parking lot with automobiles. A dense area laced with white and color resolved into a shady residential neighborhood.

This process of enlightenment and revelation continued for a couple of hours, and as the fog thinned, shrank, and flowed down the valley, I saw that there was a town beneath the white surface—that a whole world of life and activity and variety existed where I would have seen nothing but blankness had I but casually glanced and passed on.

Two thoughts came as I sat there. The first was that I had witnessed a hatching process. When I first sat, I saw nothing but the surface of a large, white egg. Soon a crack began to appear in the surface, and that crack gradually widened and the life within showed itself in ever-greater detail. As I watched, the crack opened wide enough to let out the life, and out it came, and it bustled about on its daily round. The egg became memory, but bound up in that memory was that the sun had been the heat source of the hatching process—the chicken—that had imparted form and structure out of the white nothingness and lent the energy necessary to spark the life within.

At this point, the second thought arrived. The white surface I had seen was like a piece of blank paper on which the energy of the sun—of creation—drew its forms. The shapes it finally etched out of the white void were not simply pictures, but glyphs of a language that could be understood. That house there was not merely a house or an image of a house but, specifically, the definition of a house and, by implication, the necessity for shelter, appreciation of aesthetics, construction techniques, loss of forest land, the nail industry, and so forth.

But though the implications of any given object can ultimately reach into infinity, definitions themselves—and words, which are abstractions of definitions—are limiting factors. That house across the valley, by the simple fact of its existence, limited the space it occupied from the pure abstraction of everythingness that existed prior to it being defined as a house to a specific set of responses that correspond to house. It, and the space it occupied, was house, not automobile, parking lot, grove of trees, or anything else.

What I first saw was a sea of white. White is the complete spectrum—the unification of all possibilities—and implicitly contained in the white sea were all possibilities. The creative force of the sun—the pen that wrote on this white field—wrote a certain, specific language complete with definition. Thus, it limited the space, not only with the forms themselves but with the definitions inherent in the forms. The process holds true for these words on this paper. This paper is the white field of all possibilities. I could write anything here, and the words I do write are the shapes—the factors—that limit the infinite possibilities; they are the limitations that say, "No, not poetry or fiction or article but essay."

The power of limitation through definition seems, perforce, to link the realm of ideas inextricably with the realm of the physical. There is no better example than the words on this paper. In the physical world, we have the simple fact that these words limit the amount of white space on the page by covering it up with ink, and the exact form of these physical limitations—the spaces in and between the ink—delimit the meaning a writer intends. Furthermore, we can glean certain information from a secondary limiting power of the ink on this page: its mere structure, which is simply form codified and amplified. For example, consider these samples of writing from the standpoint of structure alone:

Prose, obviously.

Rhymed couplets.

English sonnet.

In each case, the restrictions the structure has placed on the field of all possibilities have served to limit our perceptions of that space. It is now recognizable as something specific that is not, and cannot be, anything else.

The power of limitation on both the intellect and the physical, however, is actually somewhat weak. Thinkers continue to strive for intellectual understanding—read, definition—but many basic philosophic points remain arguable. Besides, ideas continue to evolve and move farther away from understanding, if for no reason other than variegation. We all agree, for instance, that a chair is to be sat on, but what does the Platonic ideal of chairness actually embody? Is it a Morris chair, a throne, or early American? Or a stone step? What is the ideal government that people should live by—democracy, totalitarianism, anarchy? What economic system? Where does economics end and politics begin?

Philosophers, politicians, critics, and pundits argue endlessly about the meanings of ideas, and that is because ideas are not easily limited by delineations and depictions of them. The problem is that, in the end, we cannot know a single fact to be universally, ultimately, and irrevocably true—apparently even the speed of light has not remained universally constant through time, nor is it precisely the same in all regions of space. Could we know such a fact, then the actual nature of the universe might eventually be deduced. Or revealed. But because perception, which is how we apprehend and know facts, is limited in range and scope—the eye can never see totality because it cannot see itself—all ideas remain in a permanent state of flux.

Likewise, the physical is not easily defined to the satisfaction of all. What, for example, is the most perfect female form? Peter Paul Rubens might answer very differently than Hugh Hefner. (Again the physical is bound with the idea.) Buckminster Fuller's house would be distinct from Frank Lloyd Wright's and both from that of a Chinese mandarin. Even the very basis of matter is indefinable since we have learned that matter is not actually something tangible but merely energy vibrating at various rates in subatomic packets, which may be either waves or particles, depending on how you view them. But while we have reduced our understanding of matter to subatomic particles, we have yet to deduce the basis of energy—the vibration—itself. Some might say it is the explosion of The Singularity at the Big Bang, while others might argue that that doesn't account for the source of the energy inherent in latent form within The Singularity. All we can say is that it was simply a state of pure Yang waiting to explode and expand into pure Yin. (Thus it is that heat death belongs to Yang and equally hot birth to Yin.)

The ultimate idea and the ultimate physical construct wrapped up together in a single state might be called, with a bit of tongue in cheek, the ultimate chicken—at once egg and creature. It would take something like that to discover a pure and accurate conception of universal truth and reality. But because it is both unconceived and inconceivable, it would seem to be impossible to apprehend. There was one additional avenue, however, down which I might pursue this chimerical being, and that avenue is emotion. What about the limiting power of definition on emotion?

Emotions, which at first glance seem impossible to define and thus limit, are, in many ways, actually more direct than the realm of the idea and more substantial than the realm of the physical. The fact that their definitions are subjective rather than objective does not negate them but actually reinforces their power, for in the proportion that something is universally known it gains significance. We can discuss an intellectual viewpoint—such as "What is the best government?"—extensively and never come to a conclusion, and if I say to you, "I live in a house," you will ask for a description. But if I tell you "I love you," you know exactly what I mean.

Although there are varying degrees and shades of love and the details of expression of love may vary from culture to culture, people from widely different backgrounds and cultures can, and do, share love and a firm understanding of what the concept means. And everyone recognizes that the basic emotion of love is at polar opposites to the basic emotion of hate. We can all feel hate at the mere mention of the word; not necessarily hatred for anything or anyone in particular, just general hate. If I say I'm unhappy, perhaps you cannot know or understand the cause of my unhappiness, but you can identify with the emotion I'm feeling. Whereas the intellectual ideal of home and the physical delineations and definitions of a house may differ from individual to individual, the loneliness of the single inhabitant of that house can be felt and empathized with by all.

The limiting power of the ways in which we delineate and recognize emotional content—such as facial expression, body language, verbal tone, and so forth—are more powerful and affecting than those for either the intellectual or the physical simply because they are more universally understood and accepted. Two enemy soldiers meeting on the battlefield need no dictionary of translation to read each other's hatred and fear. Or relief at war's end. And the ultimate proof of emotions' universal power is that they are true and authentic even for the most hardened pragmatic realist who demands that a thing be quantifiable to be actual. This is true despite the fact that emotion is somewhat akin to a singularity, which is impossible to know except by peripheral phenomenon, or to the eye, which sees everything seeable but itself.

How odd, then, that the concepts most definable—the physical and the idea—are the least susceptible to limitation, and that the concept most susceptible to limitation—emotion —is the least definable. And how interesting that, while the intellectual and the physical are occupied with scores of widely divergent possibilities, we distinguish our truly significant, basic, common human terms—emotions—only in relation to and in distinction from their opposites—again the Yin and Yang. As the song says, "There's a fine line between love and hate."

At last the hatching process was complete, and the valley was revealed. The air was clear, as if there had never been a white mist. I had sat on the steps overlooking the valley and watched as form and idea revealed themselves, but it was not the physical aspect of or the ideas contained in the revelation that had become important. Instead, it was the emotion that welled up from that ineffable place we have within us: a feeling of being at one with the mysteries of an external, idealized field of all possibility and with the mysteries within myself. And for a short time, sitting there on the stone steps overlooking the valley, I felt as if I were, at once, both chicken and egg.

Iguanas Muerte

Notes from Abroad

I WILL BE COMING BACK to Tejas in a week or so. Can't hack it here. I think I have finally gotten over the thing I had that made me want to be somewhere where nobody else was. I still want to be somewhere where nobody else is for therapeutic reasons, but where I am now there is nobody home. I used to consider this place home after I got alienated from my parents by my medulla and my genitals. I think I wouldn't have been as alienated if my parents had ever accepted that they had genitals, but they never did, so that alienated me. And when I found I was as capable of reasoning out ridiculous laws of the universe as anyone else was, and I didn't need someone else's ridiculous laws, I got alienated. From then on, I considered this to be more of a home than I considered my parents to be.

Something very predictable has happened here. When I was last here, the farms were fairly mechanized, but the people were in control of what was happening with their economics, if not their lives and medullas. Their lives and medullas were controlled by the Lutheran Church and by the church's concept of being a loyal American, which was the most important part of being a Lutheran. Now these farms are totally mechanized, but, at the same time, the farmers are no longer in control of their economic situation. This is the richest land in Norte Wespuichiland, but as far as I can tell it has become impossible to do any better than break even farming here now. They are totally in the grip of Detroit for parts for their mechanized farms, and farm machinery prices are more expensive than car parts—for example, I saw a wheel bearing for $56 and a washer sell for $15. The result, economically speaking, seems to be that they will be taking a loss from here on out and will only survive by slowly bleeding their vast savings accounts. (I am of the opinion that an average farmer in the corn belt has a savings account of $50,000–$200,000.) The thrifty ones will be able to make this last the rest of their lives, others will have to eventually sell their farms (perhaps the same progression as what happened in the Dust Bowl?). So anyway, they have very little farm labor any more, and what they have they don't pay, so I won't stay.

They have also changed from being mildly amused but friendly and open to strangers to being suspicious and hostile— as if anyone passing through was responsible for their misfortunes. Perhaps this is why Indiana, Illinois, and Ohio are such wretched states to pass through, as far as human decency is concerned, and it has just recently reached Iowa. Anyway, as I am not into repression, I am leaving for Minnesota, South Dakota, Nebraska, Colorado, and New Mexico, then down to Tejas in a few days. There is nobody home here, anyway, just a fragment of the part of Lutheranism that couldn't accept its genitals, and some tractor parts salesmen from Detroit.

See you soon,
Iguanas

Be a Poet!

YES, NOW YOU, TOO, CAN BE A POET!

Are you tired of leading a prosaic existence? Do you often wonder why poets lead such exhilarating lives and get away with dangling their participles?

It is because poets have a Poetic License. But now you, too, can enjoy this rare opportunity, thanks to our Famous Poets School. It's as simple as rhyming fish and phone.

To find out if you qualify for this amazing (never-to-be-repeated) offer, simply answer the following questions and mail to *Phosphene*. We'll decide if you have hidden talents. Let the Famous Poets School put you into the exciting new career of poetry writing!

    1. Which of the following words rhyme?
        a.) Fred
        b.) George
        c.) June
        d.) moon
    2. Complete the following rhyme:
       Hickory dickory dock,
       The mouse ran up the _____.
        a.) flagpole
        b.) street
        c.) clock
    3. Shakespeare was
        a.) a famous poet.
        b.) a laundry detergent.
        c.) a type of meatloaf.

If you answered "yes" to any of the above questions, then you are a poet and don't even know it!

Hear what our happy, satisfied customers say:

"Before I rote the Famus Poets School, I couldn't even spell, but now I rite all the tyme."

—Nancy Worsewords
London, England

"The Famous Poets School made me what I am today."

—Norman Sailor
New York, NY

"My very first haiku I sold for $40,000. Thank you Famous Poets School!"

—Jerry Richfellow
Salem, Mass.

"I used to be a ditch digger 'til I got me one of 'em Poetic Licenses. Now I writes poetry all the time while my wife does the ditches."

—Henry Welfare
Houston, Texas

Don't delay!
Mail Today!

Yes! Please rush me my very own Poetic License. On my honor I swear I took the test and didn't cheat. Enclosed also please find $1 for postage and panhandling fees.

name:

_____

address:

_____

city:

_____ state: _____ zip: _____

Offer void in states where poetry is prohibited.

More from Phosphene Publishing Company

Phosphene Publishing Company publishes books and DVDs relating to literature, history, the paranormal, film, spirituality, and the martial arts. For other great titles, visit

phosphenepublishing.com

A young state tax attorney decides to follow his dream of becoming an international photojournalist, moving with his new bride to El Salvador to cover its civil war. With the help of a few contacts, he becomes part of the freelance photographer ecosystem, going out daily to cover newsworthy events in the "low intensity conflict." Navigating an often stultifying bureaucracy, as well as the country's rugged physical terrain, he gradually adjusts to his new, often dangerous work environment. Both his professional and the war's courses evolve over a couple of years, culminating in an intersection that directly challenges his commitment to his dream.

It's World War I, and the fate of Africa lies in the hands of eccentric Royal Navy commander Geoffrey Spicer-Simson, who is ordered to destroy two ships on Lake Tanganyika that give the Germans military control over the continent. But that may be easier said than done. To get there, Spicer-Simson and his men will have to drag two 40' gunboats over desert torn with ravines, through tsetse-infested swamps, and across a 6,000-foot range of mountains. Undaunted, Spicer-Simson forges ahead, but can his men accept the leadership of a pretentious braggart who names his gunboats *Mimi* and *Toutou*, is completely covered with tattoos, and wears a leather skirt instead of a uniform? And if the journey to the lake isn't bizarre enough, imagine what happens when they get there and meet the Germans in mortal combat on the high seas in the middle of Africa! A non-fiction novel, *Lord of the Loincloth* is the humorously adventurous account of one of the 20th century's strangest heroes and his extraordinary quest for redemption.

Award-Winning Drama

It is the dawn of the 20th century, and infamous magus of black magic Aleister Crowley and poet William Butler Yeats contend for control of the Hermetic Order of the Golden Dawn. Their confrontation, based on real-life events, draws in Bram Stoker, author of Dracula, famous Irish revolutionary Maud Gonne, celebrated Victorian actress Florence Farr Emery, and mysteriously veiled author Fiona MacLeod, who is much more than she seems. Magic, seduction, and ambition collide as each strives to achieve his or her desires and dreams, until Fiona, in a prescient trance, confronts each of the others with their inner motivations and passions, sealing their fates.

As the last day of WWII unfolds inside the Sulphur Spring Inn, confused mayhem whirls around proprietor Sarah Robinson. Sarah drives her family crazy, but her ditzyness disguises a kindness big enough to cement her family together despite the heavy-handed approach of her temperamental husband, Evan, who is running for congress. To make matters worse, Evan can't stand the idea of his older daughter being courted by a soldier, but she is, and the young couple plans to wed that very day. Mixed up in the confusion is a younger daughter infatuated with a cosmopolitan older sergeant, a mischievous boy, and a wisecracking custodian. And when Sarah throws in a few bottles of Dr. Snaketoe's Lightnin' Elixir, watch out!

From a comic yet telling refiguring of August Strindberg's Miss Julie to a man discovering the daughter he never knew, these eleven Plays that Pop! explore the importance of human connections as we struggle to make the most of life. Along the way, you'll meet poet William Butler Yeats being confronted by his lost past, a woman on edge hiding a terrible secret, an army patrol facing the ultimate confusion of war, a man in airport limbo, and characters poking fun at the very notion of plays. And don't forget the missing Putty Sing! Whether you're interested in a good read or are looking for wonderful characters to people your stage, there's something here for every taste and every theater budget.

1.1 (1/2/26)

www.ingramcontent.com/pod-product-compliance
Lightning Source LLC
Chambersburg PA
CBHW060643260626
47161CB00008B/2971